World's Richest People of 21 Century

Be inspired

&

Be one of them

By Salehe .A Nantembelele

ISBN-13: 978-1518636035

To three women I love the most;

Rukia, Amne & Fatuma

This page intentionally left blank

Table of Content

This page intentionally left blank

Introduction

Probably you know something about Bill Gates, and also most probably the fact that he is the CEO of Microsoft corporation. And if not enough you might probably think that he is the richest person in the world, yeah you think that. But there are some questions that you should ask yourself. Is he realy the richest person in the world? If yes to what extent? What is his wealth? How did he get it? If no who is the richest person then? What is his/her wealth? How did he/she gett it? Who are the other richest people in the world? What is their trend from 2000 to 2014? Why did some of them go up and others go down during that period? All these questions and other are going to be answered in this book.

Apart from getting the answers to your questions this book is going to inspire you by knowing what they believe in and what are their principals in business.

Inspiration, courage, concurring fear, taking initiatives and get out of my room and kick out the so called "hard life" are some of what I have first got only from preparing this book. This is because I had to pass through details of each and every richest person I wrote about in this book. I have personally learned that they were ordinary people before and decided to change their lives. They had their principal in doing business and they lived by them. I have strong feeling that you and I can also one day be one of the richest people either in the world or our countries. It is possible, it is possible, it is possible.

You are going to learn about 20 richest people of the twenty first century to date (2000 – 2014).

Part One

In this part you will learn about top twenty richest people of the 21 century to date (2000 – 2014), their brief profile, imporntant aspects of their life and what they have to say for you.

Bill Gates

About

Brief Profile until October 2015

Born	William Henry Gates III
	October 28, 1955 (age 59)
	Seattle, Washington, U.S.
Residence	Medina, Washington, U.S.
Nationality	American
Alma mater	Harvard University (dropped out)
Occupation	Technology Advisor of Microsoft
	Co-Chair of the Bill & Melinda Gates Foundation
	CEO of Cascade Investment
	Chair of Corbis
Years active	1975–present
Net worth	US$76.5 billion (October 2015)
Board member of	Microsoft
	Berkshire Hathaway
Religion	Roman Catholicism (formerly Congregationalism)
Spouse(s)	Melinda Gates (m. 1994)
Children	3

Parent(s)	William H. Gates, Sr.
	Mary Maxwell Gates

About Bill Gates

William Henry "Bill" Gates III (born October 28, 1955) is an American business magnate, philanthropist, investor, computer programmer, and inventor. In 1975, Gates and Paul Allen co-founded Microsoft, which became the world's largest PC software company. During his career at Microsoft, Gates held the positions of chairman, CEO and chief software architect, and was the largest individual shareholder until May 2014. Gates has authored and co-authored several books.

Starting in 1987, Gates was included in the Forbes list of the world's wealthiest people and was the wealthiest overall from 1995 to 2014—excluding a few years after the Financial crisis of 2007–08. Between 2009 and 2014 his wealth doubled from US$40 billion to more than US$82B. Between 2013 and 2014 his wealth increased by US$15 billion. Gates is currently the richest man in the world.

Gates is one of the best-known entrepreneurs of the personal computer revolution. Gates has been criticized for his business tactics, which have been considered anti-competitive, an opinion which has in some cases been upheld by numerous court rulings. Later in his career Gates pursued a number of philanthropic endeavors, donating large amounts of money to various charitable organizations and scientific research programs through the Bill & Melinda Gates Foundation, established in 2000.

Gates stepped down as Chief Executive Officer of Microsoft in January 2000. He remained as Chairman and created the position of Chief Software Architect for himself. In June 2006, Gates announced that he would be transitioning from full-time work at Microsoft to part-time work, and full-time work at the Bill & Melinda Gates Foundation. He gradually transferred his duties to Ray Ozzie, chief software architect and Craig Mundie, chief research and strategy officer. Ozzie later left the company. Gates's last full-time day at Microsoft was June 27, 2008. He stepped down as Chairman of Microsoft in February 2014, taking on a new post as technology advisor to support newly appointed CEO Satya Nadella.

Sources of Income

Microsoft

Microsoft Corporation (commonly referred to as Microsoft) is an American multinational technology corporation headquartered in Redmond, Washington, that develops, manufactures, licenses, and supports computer software, consumer electronics and personal computers and services. Its best known software products are the Microsoft Windows line of operating systems, Microsoft Office office suite, and Internet Explorer and Edge web browsers. Its flagship hardware products are the Xbox game consoles and the Microsoft Surface tablet lineup. It is the world's largest software maker measured by revenues. It is also one of the world's most valuable companies.

Microsoft was founded by Paul Allen and Bill Gates on April 4, 1975, to develop and sell BASIC interpreters for Altair 8800. It rose to dominate the personal computer operating system market with MS-DOS in the mid-1980s, followed by Microsoft Windows. The company's 1986 initial public offering, and subsequent rise in its share price, created three billionaires and an estimated 12,000 millionaires from Microsoft employees. Since the 1990s, it has increasingly diversified from the operating system market and has made a number of corporate acquisitions. In May 2011, Microsoft acquired Skype Technologies for $8.5 billion in its largest acquisition to date.

As of 2015, Microsoft is market dominant in both the IBM PC-compatible operating system (while it lost the majority of the overall operating system market to Android) and office software suite markets (the latter with Microsoft Office). The company also produces a wide range of other software for desktops and servers, and is active in areas including Internet search (with Bing), the video game industry (with the Xbox, Xbox 360 and Xbox One consoles), the digital services market (through MSN), and mobile phones (via the operating systems of Nokia's former phones and Windows Phone OS). In June 2012, Microsoft entered the personal computer production market for the first time, with the launch of the Microsoft Surface, a line of tablet computers.

With the acquisition of Nokia's devices and services division to form Microsoft Mobile Oy, the company re-entered the smartphone hardware market, after its previous attempt, Microsoft Kin, which resulted from their acquisition of Danger Inc.

Microsoft is a portmanteau of the words microcomputer and software.

Bill Gates Quotes

- ✓ Success is a lousy teacher. It seduces smart people into thinking they can't lose.

- ✓ Your most unhappy customers are your greatest source of learning.

- ✓ As we look ahead into the next century, leaders will be those who empower others.

- ✓ If you can't make it good, at least make it look good.

- ✓ I really had a lot of dreams when I was a kid, and I think a great deal of that grew out of the fact that I had a chance to read a lot.

- ✓ I believe that if you show people the problems and you show them the solutions they will be moved to act.

- ✓ Technology is just a tool. In terms of getting the kids working together and motivating them, the teacher is the most important.

- ✓ If I'd had some set idea of a finish line, don't you think I would have crossed it years ago?

- ✓ Television is not real life. In real life people actually have to leave the coffee shop and go to jobs.

- ✓ Intellectual property has the shelf life of a banana.

Warren Buffett

About

Brief Profile until October 2015

Born	Warren Edward Buffett
	August 30, 1930 (age 85)
	Omaha, Nebraska, U.S.
Education	Master of Science in Economics
Alma mater	University of Nebraska–Lincoln; Columbia Business School
Occupation	Chairman & CEO of Berkshire Hathaway
Years active	1951–present
Salary	US$100,000
Net worth	US$67 billion (June 2015)
Spouse(s)	Susan Buffett (m. 1952–2004; her death)
	Astrid Menks (m. 2006)
Children	Susan Alice Buffett
	Howard Graham Buffett
	Peter Andrew Buffett

About Warren Buffett

Warren Edward Buffett (born August 30, 1930) is an American business magnate, investor and philanthropist. He is the most successful investor of the 20th century. Buffett is the chairman, CEO and largest shareholder of Berkshire Hathaway, and consistently ranked among the world's wealthiest people. He was ranked as the world's wealthiest person in 2008 and as the third wealthiest in 2015. In 2012 Time named Buffett one of the world's most influential people.

Buffett is often referred to as the "Wizard of Omaha" or "Oracle of Omaha," or the "Sage of Omaha," and is noted for his adherence to value investing and for his personal frugality despite his immense wealth. Buffett is a notable philanthropist, having pledged to give away 99 percent of his fortune to philanthropic causes, primarily via the Gates Foundation. On April 11, 2012, he was diagnosed with prostate cancer, for which he successfully completed treatment in September 2012.

Sources of Income

Berkshire Hathaway

Berkshire Hathaway Inc. is an American multinational conglomerate holding company headquartered in Omaha, Nebraska, United States. The company wholly owns GEICO, BNSF, Lubrizol, Dairy Queen, Fruit of the Loom, Helzberg Diamonds, FlightSafety International, and NetJets, owns 26% of Kraft Heinz Company and an undisclosed percentage of Mars, Incorporated, and has significant minority holdings in American Express, The Coca-Cola Company, Wells Fargo, IBM and Restaurant Brands International. Berkshire Hathaway averaged an annual growth in book value of 19.7% to its shareholders for the last 49 years (compared to 9.8% from the S&P 500 with dividends included for the same period), while employing large amounts of capital, and minimal debt.

The company is known for its control and leadership by Warren Buffett, who is the company's Chairman of the Board, President, and Chief Executive Officer, and Charlie Munger, the company's Vice-Chairman of the Board of Directors. In the early part of Buffett's career at Berkshire, he focused on long-term investments in publicly traded companies, but more recently he more frequently bought whole companies. Berkshire now owns a diverse range of businesses including confectionery, retail, railroad, home furnishings, encyclopedias, manufacturers of vacuum cleaners, jewelry sales, newspaper publishing, manufacture and distribution of uniforms, and several regional electric and gas utilities.

According to the Forbes Global 2000 list and formula, Berkshire Hathaway is the fifth largest public company in the world. On August 14, 2014, the price of the company's 'A' shares hit $200,000 per share for the first time in the history of the company.

Warren Buffett Quotes

- ✓ It takes 20 years to build a reputation and five minutes to ruin it. If you think about that, you'll do things differently.

- ✓ Price is what you pay. Value is what you get.

- ✓ It's far better to buy a wonderful company at a fair price than a fair company at a wonderful price.

- ✓ Risk comes from not knowing what you're doing.

- ✓ Someone's sitting in the shade today because someone planted a tree a long time ago.

- ✓ Rule No.1: Never lose money. Rule No.2: Never forget rule No.1.

- ✓ You only have to do a very few things right in your life so long as you don't do too many things wrong.

- ✓ It's better to hang out with people better than you. Pick out associates whose behavior is better than yours and you'll drift in that direction.

- ✓ In the business world, the rearview mirror is always clearer than the windshield.

- ✓ Our favorite holding period is forever.

Carlos Slim

About

Brief Profile until October 2015

Born	Carlos Slim Helú
	January 28, 1940 (age 75)
	Mexico City, Mexico
Residence	Mexico City, Mexico
Nationality	Mexican
Ethnicity	Lebanese
Education	Civil Engineering
Alma mater	Universidad Nacional Autónoma de México
Occupation	Chairman & CEO of Telmex, América Móvil, Samsung Mexico and Grupo Carso
Known for	World's wealthiest person (2007, 2010-2013)
Net worth	US$65.6 billion (August 2015)
Religion	Maronite Catholicism
Spouse(s)	Soumaya Domit (m. 1967; died 1999)
Children	Carlos
	Marco Antonio
	Everétt Patrick

Parent(s)	Soumaya
	Vanessa
	Johanna
	Julián Slim Haddad (deceased)
	Linda Helú

About Carlos Slim

Carlos Slim Helú (born January 28, 1940) is a Mexican business magnate, investor, and philanthropist. From 2010 to 2013, Slim was ranked as the richest person in the world. Known as the "Warren Buffett of Mexico", Slim oversees a vast business empire that is influential in every sector of the Mexican economy and accounts for 40% of the listings on the Mexican Stock Exchange. He derived his fortune from his extensive holdings in a considerable number of Mexican companies through his conglomerate, Grupo Carso. The conglomerate comprises a diverse portfolio of businesses from a wide array of industries that include telecommunications, education, health care, industrial manufacturing, food and beverages, real estate, airlines, media, mining, oil, hospitality, entertainment, technology, retail, sports and financial services. Currently, Slim is the chairman and chief executive of telecommunications companies Telmex and América Móvil.

América Móvil, which was Latin America's largest mobile-phone carrier in 2010, accounted for around $49 billion of Slim's wealth by the end of that year. As of August 2015 he is #4 on Forbes list of billionaires, and his net worth is estimated at $65.6 billion. His net worth is nearly equivalent to about 6 percent of Mexico's gross domestic product.

Sources of Income

Telmex

Telmex is a Mexican telecommunications company headquartered in Mexico City that provides telecommunications products and services in Mexico, Argentina, Chile, Colombia, Brazil (Embratel),

11

Ecuador, Peru, Venezuela and other countries in Latin America. Telmex is still the dominant fixed-line phone carrier in Mexico. In addition to traditional fixed-line telephone service, Telmex offers Internet access, data, hosted services and IPTV. Telmex owns 90 percent of the telephone lines in Mexico City and 80 percent of the lines in the country. Telmex is a wholly owned subsidiary of América Móvil.

América Móvil

América Móvil is a Mexican telecommunications corporation headquartered in Mexico City, Mexico. It is the fourth largest mobile network operator in terms of equity subscribers and one of the largest corporations in the world. América Móvil is a Forbes Global 2000 company. A venture of Carlos Slim, América Móvil provides services to 289.4 million wireless subscribers, 34.3 million landlines, 22.6 million broadband accesses and 21.5 million PayTV units as of the end of 2014.

Grupo Carso

Grupo Carso or Grupo Sanborns SAB is a global conglomerate company owned by Carlos Slim. It was formed in 1990 after the merger of Corporación Industrial Carso and Grupo Inbursa. The name Carso stands for Carlos Slim and Soumaya Domit de Slim, his late wife.

In May 2014, the conglomerate had a stock market capitalisation of over $12 billion US dollars.

In 1996 Carso Global Telecom (which includes Telmex, Telcel and América Móvil) separated itself from Grupo Carso.

Carlos Slim Quotes

✓ Competition makes you better, always, always makes you better, even if the competitor wins.

✓ If you're in business, you need to understand the environment. You need to have a vision of the future, and you need to know the past.

✓ Mistakes are normal and human. Make them small, accept them, correct them, and forget them.

✓ Firm and patient optimism always yields its rewards.

✓ I don't believe too much in luck. I believe in circumstances. I believe in work.

✓ Any personal crisis—you have to use it to get stronger.

✓ Do not allow negative feelings and emotions to control your mind. Emotional harm does not come from others; it is conceived and developed within ourselves.

✓ All businesses make mistakes. The trick is to avoid large ones.

✓ When we face our problems, they disappear. So learn from failure and let success be the silent incentive.

✓ You have to have an international reference of competition. You have to go beyond your home.

Larry Ellison

About

Brief Profile until October 2015

Born	August 17, 1944 (age 71)
	Lower East Side, Manhattan, New York, U.S.
Residence	Woodside, California, U.S.
Nationality	American
Alma mater	University of Illinois at Urbana-Champaign (dropped out)
	University of Chicago (dropped out)
Occupation	Executive Chairman and CTO of Oracle Corporation
Known for	Co-founder and CEO of Oracle Corporation
Salary	$77 million (2013)
Net worth	US$50 billion (June 2015)
Spouse(s)	Adda Quinn (m. 1967; div. 1974)
	Nancy Wheeler Jenkins (m. 1977; div. 1978)
	Barbara Boothe (m. 1983; div. 1986)
	Melanie Craft (m. 2003; div. 2010)
Children	David Ellison
	Megan Ellison

About Larry Ellison

Lawrence Joseph "Larry" Ellison (born August 17, 1944) is an American internet entrepreneur, businessman and philanthropist. He serves as executive chairman and chief technology officer of Oracle Corporation, having previously been chief executive from its founding until September 2014. In 2014, he was listed by Forbes as the third-wealthiest man in America and as the fifth-wealthiest person in the world, with a fortune of $56.2 billion.

Ellison was born in New York City but grew up in Chicago. He studied at the University of Illinois at Urbana–Champaign and the University of Chicago without graduating before moving to California in 1966. While working at Ampex in the early 1970s, he became influenced by Edgar F. Codd's research on relational database design, which led in 1977 to the formation of what became Oracle. Oracle became a successful database vendor to mid- and low-range systems, competing with Sybase and Microsoft SQL Server, which led to Ellison being listed by Forbes as the richest Californian in 2006.

Ellison has donated up to 1% of his wealth to charity and has signed The Giving Pledge. In addition to his work at Oracle, Ellison has had success in yachting, through Oracle Team USA, and is a licensed aircraft pilot who owns two military jets.

Sources of Income

Oracle Corporation

The Oracle Corporation is an American global computer technology corporation, headquartered in Redwood City, California. The company primarily specializes in developing and marketing computer hardware systems and enterprise software products – particularly its own brands of database management systems. In 2011 Oracle was the second-largest software maker by revenue, after Microsoft.

The company also develops and builds tools for database development and systems of middle-tier software, enterprise resource planning (ERP) software, customer relationship management (CRM) software and supply chain management (SCM) software.

Larry Ellison, a co-founder of Oracle, served as Oracle's CEO from founding. On September 18, 2014, it was announced that he would be stepping down (with Mark Hurd and Safra Catz to become CEOs). Ellison became executive chairman and CTO. He also served as the Chairman of the Board until his replacement by Jeffrey O. Henley in 2004. On August 22, 2008, the Associated Press ranked Ellison as the top-paid chief executive in the world.

Larry Ellison Quotes

- ✓ Life's a journey. It's a journey about discovering limits.

- ✓ Great achievers are driven, not so much by the pursuit of success, but by the fear of failure.

- ✓ When you innovate, you've got to be prepared for people telling you that you are nuts. – Larry Ellison

- ✓ You have to believe in what you do in order to get what you want.

- ✓ You have to act and act now.

- ✓ To model yourself after Steve Jobs is like, 'I'd like to paint like Picasso, what should I do? Should I use more red?'

- ✓ If you do everything that everyone else does in business, you're going to lose. The only way to really be ahead, is to 'be different'.

- ✓ I'm addicted to winning. The more you win, the more you want to win.

- ✓ There's a wonderful saying that's dead wrong. 'Why did you climb the mountain?' 'I climbed the mountain because it was there.' That's utter nonsense...You climbed the mountain because you were there, and you were curious if you could do it. You wondered what it would be like.

- ✓ When I started Oracle, what I wanted to do was to create an environment where I would enjoy working. That was my primary goal. Sure, I wanted to make a living. I certainly never expected to become rich, certainly not this rich. I mean, rich does not even describe this. This is surreal. And it has nothing to do with money. I mean, you buy clothes with money, and cars. But I really wanted to work with people I enjoyed working with, who I admired and liked.

✓ When you live your life in different ways, it makes people around you become uncomfortable. So deal with it. They don't know what you are going to do.

✓ When you are the first person whose beliefs are different from what everyone else believes, you are basically saying, 'I'm right and everyone else is wrong.' That's a very unpleasant position to be in. It's at once exhilaration and the same time an invitation to be attacked.

✓ You can't spend as much money as I have, even if you try. I've been trying.

✓ The only way to get ahead is to find errors in conventional wisdom.

✓ I believe people have to follow their dreams—I did.

✓ When I do something, it is all about self-discovery. I want to learn and discover my own limits.

✓ I have had all the disadvantages required for success.

Amancio Ortega

About

Brief Profile until October 2015

Born	Amancio Ortega Gaona
	28 March 1936 (age 79)
	Busdongo de Arbás, León, Spain
Residence	A Coruña, Spain
Nationality	Spanish
Occupation	Businessman
Known for	Co-founder of the Inditex group
Net worth	US$70.9 billion (August 2015)
Board member of	Inditex (CEO) Daez (COO)
Religion	Roman Catholicism.
Spouse(s)	Rosalía Mera (divorced)
	Flora Pérez Marcote (m. 2001)
Children	Sandra Ortega Mera
	Marcos Ortega Mera
	Marta Ortega Pérez

About Amancio Ortega

The youngest of four children, Ortega was born in Busdongo de Arbás, León, Spain, and spent his childhood in León. He left school and moved to La Coruña at the age of 14, due to the job of his father, a railway worker. Shortly after, he found a job as a shop hand for a local shirtmaker called Gala, which still sits on the same corner in downtown A Coruña, and learnt to make clothes by hand. In 1972, he founded Confecciones Goa (his initials in reverse), selling quilted bathrobes which Ortega produced using thousands of local women organised into sewing cooperatives. In 1975, he opened his first Zara store, so called because his preferred name Zorba was already taken. He opened many big Zara Stores during the eighties throughout Galicia. Today, Zara is part of the Inditex group (Industrias de Diseño Textil Sociedad Anónima), of which Ortega owns 59.29%, and aside from over 6,000 stores includes the brands Zara, Massimo Dutti, Oysho, Zara Home, Kiddy's Class, Tempe, Stradivarius, Pull and Bear, Bershka and has more than 92,000 employees.

Ortega keeps a very low profile and, until 1999, no photograph of Ortega had ever been published and is known for his preference for a simple lifestyle. He refuses to wear a tie and typically wears a simple uniform of a blue blazer, white shirt, and gray pants, none of which are Zara products. He is also said to take a very active part in the production and design process in the company.

When he made a public appearance in 2000 as part of the warm-up prior to his company's initial public offering on the stock market in 2001, it made headlines in the Spanish financial press. However, he has only granted interviews to three journalists ever and his secrecy has led to the publication of books, such as Amancio Ortega: de cero a Zara (From Zero to Zara).

In 2011, Ortega announced his imminent retirement from Inditex, parent company of the Zara chain, stating that he would ask Inditex vice-president and CEO Pablo Isla to take his place at the helm of the textile empire.

Sources of Income

Inditex Group

Industria de Diseño Textil, S.A. (Inditex) Spanish: (Textile Design Industries) is a Spanish multinational clothing company headquartered in Arteixo, Galicia. It is made up of almost a hundred companies dealing in activities related to textile design, production, and distribution. Amancio Ortega, Spain's richest man, and currently the world's fourth richest man, is the founder and current largest shareholder. The current chairman of Inditex is Pablo Isla.

Inditex, the biggest fashion group in the world, operates over 6,600 stores worldwide and owns brands like Massimo Dutti, Bershka, Oysho, Pull and Bear, Stradivarius, Zara, Tempe, and Uterqüe, and also a low-cost brand Lefties. The majority of its stores are corporate-owned; franchises are only conceded in countries where corporate properties can not be foreign-owned (in some Middle Eastern countries, for example).

The group designs and manufactures almost everything by itself, and new designs are dispatched twice a week to Zara stores.

Most of the company's manufacturing is done in countries with low labour costs, mainly in Morocco, China and Turkey, although some production continues in Spain and Portugal, particularly for its Zara brand. In addition, Inditex has a factory for shoe design, production and distribution in the town of Elche, on the Spanish Mediterranean coast.

Amancio Ortega Quotes

✓ Die of success? Give me a break! We've only just started!

✓ The customer has always driven the business model...

✓ I am the property of my business, not the reverse.

✓ You must appear three times in the newspapers: when you are born, when you get married, and when you die.

✓ The problem of succession in businesses anywhere in the world arises from the fact that not all legal heirs are suitable.

✓ We cannot limit ourselves to continuing on the path we have already opened...

✓ Once again we will have to be enthusiastic and exacting in order to convert ideas and projects into reality...

- ✓ Attempt to seduce the customer with the latest fashion, the finest design, and the most attentive service.

- ✓ [In 2004 when it had just reached 2,000 sales outlets] Inditex's strategic plan foresees a total of 4,000 stores in the next five years…

- ✓ One thing hasn't changed – the innovative spirit and urge for improvement that was the driving force back then.

- ✓ The key part of Inditex's business model is its human capital.

- ✓ Companies are comprised of human beings without the effort, professionalisms and motivation of whom, no achievement could be made.

- ✓ Innovation and commitment towards our customers define our corporate culture…

- ✓ We must be able to retain talent, keep our staff motivated and recruit new individuals in the company at a fast pace, and to achieve at the same time for the company a fresh look and the required ambition to be the driving force enabling us to meet new and ambitious purposes.

- ✓ The motivation of almost 90,000 individuals working towards a single objective…

- ✓ Store employees have the best understanding of… customer tastes…

- ✓ Putting our capacity for profitable growth in the long term to the scrutiny of investors.

- ✓ We had the certainty of a philosophy and a business culture capable of facing up to the challenges which were arising.

- ✓ The future will be marked by the result of combining the flow of accumulated experience with the youth of those who, day by day, join the Group, and these ingredients are going to make it possible for us to continue to this great project forward with the confidence of the first day.

✓ We must be aware that the experience we have gained is not enough to guarantee our leadership. We must also be faithful to the commitment to effort and improvement which inspires our company.

✓ More than 12,000 people from many different countries currently make up our group. This diversity is synonymous with open-mindedness and flexibility, and pushes us to continue evolving, with enthusiasm and perseverance, towards new projects.

✓ International expansion, carried out both independently and through agreements with other companies, is the objective that cannot be delayed and will allow us, through diversity, to enrich our culture and vision of the market.

✓ The creation of new chains and the widening of our product ranges is our response to the new opportunities of the environment.

✓ Innovation and constant improvement... must keep on being the motivating idea of our Group throughout the 21st century.

✓ The international expansion of the group in 1999 has continued at an intense rate. Inditex is present in already thirty countries, nine more than the previous year.

✓ Business efficiency is... an expression of the quality of the management of our business, the complex network of activities of a vertically integrated fashion distribution group, which designs, produces and sells in three continents.

✓ The future of Inditex is tied to our capacity to respond day by day to the demands of the market and to design and set in motion new projects which are capable of connecting with the desires of our clients around the world.

✓ We cannot limit ourselves to continuing on the path we have already opened and once again we will have to be enthusiastic and exacting in order to convert ideas and projects into reality in a world that is advancing at great speed.

Lakshmi Mittal

About

Brief Profile until October 2015

Born	15 June 1950 (age 65)
	Sadulpur, Rajasthan, India
Residence	London, United Kingdom
Nationality	Indian
Alma mater	St. Xavier's College, Kolkata, (B.Com.)
Occupation	Chairman & CEO of ArcelorMittal
	Owner of Karrick Limited
	Co-owner of
	Queens Park Rangers F.C.
Known for	Acquiring and turning around sick steel-mills, King of Steel, Steel tycoon
Net worth	Decrease US$ 10.3 billion (September 2015)
Board member of	Goldman Sachs
	EADS
Spouse(s)	Usha Mittal
Children	Vanisha Mittal
	Aditya Mittal

About Lakshmi Mittal

Lakshmi Niwas Mittal (born 15 June 1950) is an Indian steel magnate, based in the United Kingdom. He is the chairman and CEO of ArcelorMittal, the world's largest steelmaking company. Mittal owns 38% of ArcelorMittal and holds a 34% stake in Queens Park Rangers F.C..

In 2007, Mittal was considered to be the richest Hindu and Asian person in Europe. Despite being the eighth wealthiest man in Britain in 2002, he does not hold British citizenship. He was ranked the sixth richest person in the world by Forbes in 2011, but dropped to 82nd place in March 2015. In spite of the drop, Forbes estimated that he still had a personal wealth of US$16 billion in October 2013. He is also the 57th "most powerful person" of the 72 individuals named in Forbes' "Most Powerful People" list for 2015. His daughter Vanisha Mittal's wedding was the second most expensive in recorded history.

Mittal has been a member of the board of directors of Goldman Sachs since 2008, and is also member of the board of directors of the European Aeronautic Defence and Space Company (EADS). He sits on the World Steel Association's executive committee, and is a member of the Indian Prime Minister's Global Advisory Council, the Foreign Investment Council in Kazakhstan, the World Economic Forum's International Business Council, and the Presidential International Advisory Board of Mozambique. He also sits on the advisory board of Northwestern University's Kellogg School of Management in the United States and is a member of the board of trustees of the Cleveland Clinic.

In 2006 The Sunday Times named him "Business Person of 2006", the Financial Times named him "Person of the Year", and Time magazine named him "International Newsmaker of the Year 2006". In 2007, Time magazine included him in their "100 most influential persons in the world".

Sources of Income

ArcelorMittal

ArcelorMittal was created by the takeover of Western European steel maker Arcelor (Spain, France, and Luxembourg) by Indian-owned multinational steel maker Mittal Steel in 2006, at a cost of €40.37 per share, approximately $33 billion total. Mittal Steel launched a hostile takeover bid which replaced a previous planned merger between Arcelor and Severstal, which had lacked sufficient shareholder approval. The resulting merged business was named ArcelorMittal and is headquartered in Luxembourg.

The resulting firm produced approximately 10% of the world's steel, and was by far the world's largest steel company. Total revenues in 2007 were $105 billion. In October 2008, the market capitalisation of ArcelorMittal was over $30 billion.

Mittal Steel Company

Mittal Steel Company N.V. was one of the world's largest steel producers by volume, and also one of the largest in turnover. The company is now part of ArcelorMittal.

CEO Lakshmi Mittal's family owned 88% of the company. Mittal Steel was based in Rotterdam but managed from London by Mittal and his son Aditya. It was formed when Ispat International N.V. acquired LNM Holdings N.V. (both were already controlled by Lakshmi Mittal) and merged with International Steel Group Inc. (the remnants of Bethlehem Steel, Republic Steel and LTV Steel) in 2004. On 25 June 2006, Mittal Steel decided to takeover Arcelor, with the new company to be called ArcelorMittal. The takeover has been successfully approved by shareholders and directors of Arcelor making L.N. Mittal the largest steel maker in the world.

Lakshmi Mittal Quotes

✓ When people can see which direction the leaders are going in it becomes easier to motivate them.

✓ It is true that we are interested in scale but there are very sound reasons for this.

✓ Everyone experiences tough times, it is a measure of your determination and dedication how you deal with them and how you can come through them.

✓ Hard work certainly goes a long way. These days a lot of people work hard, so you have to make sure you work even harder and really dedicate yourself to what you are doing and setting out to achieve.

✓ It's difficult for them to do a deal at these levels.

✓ At the end of the day you have to keep emotions away.

✓ Production cutbacks have remained in place in the third quarter and this has helped to further reduce inventory levels worldwide,

✓ We do not believe in oversupplying the market. When you are a large company, you can afford to do it. When you are a small player, your flexibility gets reduced.

✓ This is not about creating a giant. It's about creating the sustainability of the steel industry.

✓ We are pleased with the very positive reception our offer has received, and are confident that progress is being made towards establishing the regulatory framework for the offer.

✓ I understand that this has taken a lot of politicians by surprise. But we believe that this is an important and right step for the steel industry.

✓ In the past twenty years, we have lived through several cycles and we have always managed to buy under good terms and conditions at the right time. This has enabled us to build a solid group that is now the world number one.

✓ I am sure all politicians will be convinced of the merits of this deal.

✓ It's true that I run a multi-national group but I have no interests in India. So please tell me, what should my identity be?

✓ There will be no job cuts arising out of this merger in Europe — this is in the interest of jobs in Europe.

- ✓ I have confidence that the government of Luxembourg will not make any decision that frustrates this transaction.

- ✓ If I go to a match it doesn't mean I want to buy the stadium or the club.

- ✓ We have no intention of shutting down plants. We have always said there will be no redundancies or lay-offs as a result of this merger.

- ✓ This is a learning in the business life that first of all you need to have commitment, dedication and passion for what you are doing.

- ✓ It is a high for me. It is my biggest and most satisfying deal,

- ✓ When I think about parallels between myself and an Olympian, I believe that success in the world of business is underpinned by very similar principles of perseverance and hard work.

- ✓ I built a steel plant from the grassroots, so I learned all the nuts and bolts. When there was a problem, I would be able to guide them, though I am not a technical person.

- ✓ We are beginning to see the benefits of global consolidation,

- ✓ I'm cautious about the currency situation, oil pricing and the economies of some countries not performing as we are expecting.

- ✓ We are not in the business of iron ore. Whatever captive iron ore sources we have, we use it to make steel

- ✓ A strong player, which has the sufficient critical mass, can withhold pressure better and create a more stable environment that benefits shareholders as well as employees.

- ✓ I am very confident that we will be able to convince all the stakeholders – the shareholders, the governments and the employees, that this is in their best interests.

✓ Always think outside the box and embrace opportunities that appear, wherever they might be.

✓ We have experienced highly challenging global market conditions in the past quarter with significant steel price decline in all regions.

✓ The danger, though – and there have been signs of this recently – is that Europe begins to demonstrate a return to more nationalist sentiment. To my mind, that would be a great mistake.

✓ In our industry today only a strong company with a global reach can ensure long-term employment and provide acceptable returns for shareholders.

Bernard Arnault

About

Brief Profile until October 2015

Born	Bernard Jean Étienne Arnault
	5 March 1949 (age 66)
	Roubaix, France
Residence	Paris, France
Nationality	France
Alma mater	École Polytechnique
Occupation	Chairman & CEO of LVMH
	Chairman of Christian Dior S.A.
Net worth	US$38.9 billion (June 2015)
Religion	Roman Catholic
Spouse(s)	Anne Dewavrin (m. 1973–1990)
	Hélène Mercier (m. 1991)
Children	5, including Delphine Arnault
	Antoine Arnault

About Bernard Arnault

Bernard Jean Étienne Arnault (born 5 March 1949) is a French business magnate, investor. philanthropist and art collector. He is the chairman and Chief Executive Officer of LVMH since 1989. In March 2015, Forbes estimated his wealth to be $37 billion, making him the 13th richest person in the world and the richest in France.

His father Jean Leon Arnault was a manufacturer and the owner of a civil engineering company, Ferret-Savinel. After graduating from the Maxence Van Der Meersch High School in Roubaix, Bernard Arnault was admitted to the École Polytechnique (X1969) from which he graduated with degree in engineering in 1971.

After graduation, in 1971, he joined his father's company. In 1976, he convinced his father to liquidate the construction division of the company for 40 million French francs, and to change the focus of the company to real estate. Using the name Férinel, the new company developed a specialty in holiday accommodation. Named director of company development in 1974, he became the CEO three years later. In 1979, he succeeded his father as president of the company.

Sources of Income

LVMH

LVMH Moët Hennessy Louis Vuitton SE, better known as LVMH, is a French multinational luxury goods conglomerate, headquartered in Paris. The company was formed by the 1987 merger of fashion house Louis Vuitton with Moët Hennessy, a company formed after the 1971 merger between the champagne producer Moët & Chandon and Hennessy, the cognac manufacturer. It controls around 60 subsidiaries that each manage a small number of prestigious brands. The subsidiaries are often managed independently. The oldest of the LVMH brands is wine producer Château d'Yquem, which dates its origins back to 1593.

Christian Dior, the luxury goods group, is the main holding company of LVMH, owning 40.9% of its shares, and 59.01% of its voting rights. Bernard Arnault, majority shareholder of Dior, is Chairman of both companies and CEO of LVMH. Arnault's successful integration of various famous aspirational brands into the group has inspired other luxury companies into doing the same. Thus, the French conglomerate Kering (formerly named PPR) and the Swiss-based Richemont have also created extended portfolios of luxury brands.

Bernard Arnault Quotes

✓ A good product can last forever.

✓ Vuitton has always been a pioneer.

✓ We're the only group that has the ability to manage different activities that cover the entire range of the luxury business.

✓ In order to be able to sell a product at a relatively high price, you have to offer the craftsmanship and quality that goes along with it.

✓ One does not invite a thousand guests to watch a procession of dresses which could be seen on a coat hanger or in a show room.

✓ My relationship to luxury goods is really very rational. It is the only area in which it is possible to make luxury profit margins.

✓ We have unique products.

✓ Our strategy is to trust the creators.

✓ We don't like failures.

✓ Designers are closer to artists than to engineers.

✓ Every time there's been a crisis, we've gained market share.

✓ We do not put the entire company at risk by introducing all new products all the time.

✓ Sometimes you do not succeed.

✓ We learned that genius is not enough to succeed.

✓ The key to success is this duality – timelessness and the utmost modernity.

✓ It is not enough to have a talented designer; the management must be inspired too. The creative process is very disorganized; the production process has to be very rational.

31

✓ If you deeply appreciate and love what creative people do and how they think, which is usually in unpredictable and irrational ways, then you can start to understand them. And finally, you can see inside their minds and DNA.

✓ In the luxury business you have to build on heritage. On brands, on history… It's not an easy business, it's a business of passion that takes time. But when it's done right the potential is enormous.

✓ I like that combination between creativity and the creative process and the organization needed to make a business like this successful worldwide.

✓ Most competitors prefer to show off-mass produced clothing on their catwalks, or indulge in American-style marketing. We are not interested in working this way.

✓ Products which are customer driven are usually not innovative. Consequently, it is difficult to charge a premium.

✓ You will never be able to predict the success of a product… Obviously we won't launch a product if the tests clearly show it is going to be a failure, but we won't use tests to modify products, either… Our strategy is to trust the creators. You have to give them leeway. When creative team believes in a product, you have to trust the team's gut instinct.

✓ A star brand is current or you would call it fashionable. It is edgy, it has sex appeal, it is modern. In some way, it fulfils a fantasy. It is so new and unique, you want to buy it. You feel as if you must buy it, in fact, or else you won't be in the moment. You will be left behind.

✓ We don't like failures. We try to avoid them. That is why with many of our products, we make a limited number. We do not put the entire company at risk by introducing all new products all the time. In any given year in fact, only 15% of our business comes from the new; the rest comes from traditional, proven products – the classics.

- ✓ Choosing a creator is always difficult. It's not a question of taking a talented creator and saying, 'We'll employ the person in such and such a business and it will work'. It isn't true. It's far more complicated. We need to find the talent, the ideas and the personality that can adapt to the spirit, the history of the brand.

- ✓ When something has to be done, do it! In France we are full of good ideas, but we rarely put them into practice.

- ✓ Star brand is timeless, modern, fast growing, and highly profitable.

- ✓ They saw it was working. And then they said, 'Okay, now we are going to do the same thing.' I think, really, they underestimate the difficulty. They underestimate the time required to make it successful. And my guess is that they will have a very tough time.

- ✓ China is the most interesting part of the world for me now. I go there two or three times a year, most recently in Dalian, where we've just opened in a new mall. There are so many people who are getting to the stage where they want to consume, who want to be part of a club.

- ✓ China is feeling the effects of the crisis, but less than the U.S. And when you consider that Chinese tourists are now buying as much as Japanese tourists, when there were virtually none just 10 years ago, I'm not so worried.

- ✓ It gives people working at the group a feeling that they don't exist only for cash flow, but for something bigger.

Karl Albrecht

About

Brief Profile until October 2015

Born	Karl Hans Albrecht
	20 February 1920
	Essen, Rhine Province, Weimar Republic
Died	16 July 2014 (aged 94) Essen, Germany
Ethnicity	German
Occupation	Entrepreneur
Known for	Co-founder of Aldi
Net worth	IncreaseUS$29 billion (2014)
Religion	Catholic
Spouse(s)	Mia Tenbrink (1923–2013)
Children	Karl Albrecht junior (de) (born 1948), Beate Heister

About Karl Albrecht

Karl Hans Albrecht (20 February 1920 – 16 July 2014) was a German entrepreneur who founded the discount supermarket chain Aldi with his brother Theo. He was for many years the richest person in Germany. As of February 2014, he was ranked as 21st-richest person in the world by Hurun Report.

Karl and Theo Albrecht were born and raised in modest circumstances in Essen, Germany. Their father, Karl Sr, was employed as a miner and later as a baker's assistant. Their mother Anna, née Siepmann, had a small grocery store in the worker's quarter of Schonnebeck (de), a suburb of Essen. Theo completed an apprenticeship in his mother's store, while Karl worked in a delicatessen shop. Karl served in the Wehrmacht during World War II and was wounded on the Eastern Front. After the war, the brothers jointly took over their mother's business and founded Albrecht KG. They separated that company in 1961 into Aldi Nord, covering the part of Germany north of the Ruhr under Theo Albrecht, and Aldi Süd under Karl. The first Aldi (short for Albrecht Discount) was opened in 1962.

In 1994, Karl Albrecht removed himself from the daily operations of Aldi Süd and took the position of chairman of the board until 2002. At the beginning of 2002, he also relinquished this position, thereby completely ceding control of the firm. Today, the business is no longer run by any of Karl Albrecht's family members.

Sources of Income

Aldi

Aldi (stylized as ALDI) is a leading global discount supermarket chain with over 10,000 stores in 18 countries, and an estimated turnover of more than €50bn. Based in Germany, the chain was founded by brothers Karl and Theo Albrecht in 1946 when they took over their father's store in Essen which had been in operation since 1913; it is one of the world's largest privately owned companies. The brothers built up a chain of stores until, by 1960, they owned 300 shops, and split the operation into two separate groups, that later became Aldi Nord, headquartered in Essen; and Aldi Süd, headquartered in Mülheim an der Ruhr. The two operate independently, each within specific areas. In 1962 they introduced the name ALDI (a syllabic abbreviation for Albrecht Diskont), which is pronounced ['aldi:] (listen) in German. Aldi Nord and Aldi Süd have been financially and legally separate since 1966, although both divisions' names may appear (as if they were a single enterprise) with certain house brands or when negotiating with contractor companies. The formal business name is Aldi Einkauf GmbH & Compagnie, oHG.

The individual groups were originally owned and managed by brothers Karl Albrecht and Theo Albrecht. Karl Albrecht (d. 2014) retained ownership of Aldi Süd, and with a personal wealth of

€17.2 billion, making him the richest man in Germany, while the co-owners of Aldi Nord, Berthold and Theo Albrecht Jr., close behind at €16 billion. Dieter Schwarz, owner of Lidl and Kaufland came in third, with a fortune of €11.5 billion.

Aldi's German operations consist of Aldi Nord's 35 individual regional companies with about 2,500 stores in western, northern, and Eastern Germany, and Aldi Süd's 32 regional companies with 1,600 stores in western and southern Germany.

Internationally, Aldi Nord operates in Denmark, France, the Benelux countries, the Iberian peninsula, and Poland, while Aldi Süd operates in Ireland, United Kingdom, Hungary, Switzerland, Australia, Austria and Slovenia (Aldi Süd operates as Hofer within the latter two countries mentioned). Both Aldi Nord and Aldi Süd also operate in the United States; Aldi Nord is owner of the Trader Joe's chain, while Aldi Süd operates as Aldi.

In December 2002, a survey conducted by the German market research institute Forsa, 95% of blue-collar workers, 88% of white-collar workers, 84% of public servants, and 80% of self-employed Germans shop at Aldi. One of Aldi's direct competitors internationally is Lidl

Karl Albrecht Quotes

- ✓ If you're not serving the customer, you'd better be serving someone who is.

- ✓ Change your language and you change your thoughts.

- ✓ Start out with an ideal and end up with a deal.

- ✓ Change your language and you change your thoughts.

- ✓ If the frontline people do count, you couldn't prove it by examining the reward systems in most organizations.

- ✓ If you're not serving the customer, you'd better be serving someone who is.

- ✓ Start out with an ideal and end up with a deal.

✓ Customer needs have an unsettling way of not staying satisfied for very long.

✓ Albrecht's Law - Intelligent people, when assembled into an organization, will tend toward collective stupidity.

✓ The typical human life seems to be quite unplanned, undirected, unlived, and unsavored. Only those who consciously think about the adventure of living as a matter of making choices among options, which they have found for themselves, ever establish real self-control and live their lives fully.

Paul Allen

About

Brief Profile until October 2015

Born	Paul Gardner Allen
	January 21, 1953 (age 62)
	Seattle, Washington, U.S.
Residence	Mercer Island, Washington, U.S.
Education	Lakeside School
Alma mater	Washington State University (dropped out in 1974)
Occupation	Philanthropist, investor, entrepreneur, author, sports owner, guitarist, filmmaker, explorer, neuroscience supporter and space pioneer
Known for	Chairman and founder Vulcan Inc.
	Owner Seattle Seahawks and Portland Trail Blazers
	Part-owner Seattle Sounders
	Founder Allen Institute for Brain Science
	Founder Allen Institute for Cell Science
	Founder Allen Institute for Artificial Intelligence
	Co-founder Microsoft
	1× Super Bowl Champion (XLVIII)

	2× NFC Champion (2013, 2014)
Net worth	Increase US$17.9 billion (September 2015)
Parent(s)	Kenneth Sam Allen
	Edna Faye Allen

About Paul Allen

Paul Gardner Allen (born January 21, 1953) is an American philanthropist, investor, musician, and innovator, best known as the co-founder of Microsoft alongside Bill Gates. As of July 2015, he was estimated to be the 51st richest person in the world, with an estimated wealth of $17.5 billion.

Allen is the founder and chairman of Vulcan Inc., which manages his various business and philanthropic efforts. Allen also has a multibillion-dollar investment portfolio including technology companies, real estate holdings, and stakes in other technology and media companies. He owns two professional sports teams, the Seattle Seahawks of the National Football League (NFL), and the Portland Trail Blazers of the National Basketball Association (NBA) and is part-owner of the Seattle Sounders FC, which joined Major League Soccer (MLS) in 2009.

He is also the founder of the Allen Institute for Brain Science, the Allen Institute for Artificial Intelligence, the Allen Institute for Cell Science and Vulcan Aerospace.

Sources of Income

Microsoft

See page 5

Paul Allen Quotes

✓ I've really enjoyed being the owner of the Trail Blazers. I've tried hard to bring the city a championship. Now we are in a tough rebuilding process with a broken financial model. We have asked for help in fixing it. If I have to sell the team or if it can't continue, that will be sad.

✓ We believe Tim will solidify the football culture of the Seahawks,

✓ When it comes to helping out, I don't believe in doing it for the media attention. My goal is to support the organizations that need help.

✓ Incredible feeling of emptiness. It's a missed opportunity.

✓ It just didn't work out here. I'll have great memories. There were some amazing games.

✓ In my own work, I've tried to anticipate what's coming over the horizon, to hasten its arrival, and to apply it to people's lives in a meaningful way.

✓ The possible is constantly being redefined, and I care deeply about helping humanity move forward.

✓ Being an active board member for a dynamic and successful company such as Microsoft is a time-intensive role and one I have enjoyed for many years. However, this new role will enable me to spend my time on technology and products, where I can really make a significant contribution.

✓ The millwrights have done a wonderful job of restoration,

✓ There's an incredible feeling of emptiness and missed opportunity.

✓ There's a good chance of getting my original investment paid back, ... That's pretty amazing.

✓ We've had some tough times, but we've hung in there.

✓ Operating revenues from the Rose Garden -- including all the revenues from suites, club seats, concessions and other sources -- had become insufficient to pay the heavy debt burden, due, in large part, to declining attendance.

✓ Its incredible. I'm just really happy for the fans and the community. Everybody has supported the team all these years. And this year has been a special year n especially for the fans and the community.

✓ This just feels like a different year, and that turned out to be the case today. Just the unity you feel here in the locker room. The amount of support you hear from the fans. It's just a different year.

Ingvar Kamprad

About

Brief Profile until October 2015

Born	30 March 1926 (age 89)
	Älmhult, Sweden
Occupation	Founder of IKEA
Net worth	US$3.5 billion (Forbes, June 2015)
Spouse(s)	Kerstin Wadling (1950-1960; divorced)
	Margaretha Stennert (1960s-2011, her death)
Children	Peter, Jonas, Mathias (Stennert)
	Annika Kihlbom (Wadling, adopted)

About Ingvar Kamprad

Ingvar Feodor Kamprad born (30 March 1926) is a Swedish business magnate. He is the founder of IKEA, a Swedish retail company specialising in furniture, and is one of the richest people in the world.

Kamprad was born in Pjätteryd (now part of Älmhult Municipality), Sweden. He was raised on a farm called Elmtaryd (presently standardized Älmtaryd) near the small village of Agunnaryd in Ljungby Municipality in the province of Småland. His paternal grandfather was from Germany, but moved the family to Sweden.

Kamprad began to develop a business as a young boy, selling matches to neighbors from his bicycle. He found that he could buy matches in bulk very cheaply from Stockholm, sell them individually at a low price, and still make a good profit. From matches, he expanded to selling fish, Christmas tree decorations, seeds, and later ballpoint pens and pencils. When Kamprad was 17, his father gave him a cash reward for succeeding in his studies.

IKEA was founded in 1943 at Kamprad's uncle Ernst's kitchen table. In 1948, Kamprad diversified his portfolio, adding furniture. His business was mostly mail-order. The acronym IKEA is made up of the initials of his name (Ingvar Kamprad) plus those of Elmtaryd, the family farm where he was born, and the nearby village Agunnaryd.

In June 2013, Kamprad resigned from the board of Inter IKEA Holding SA and his youngest son Mathias Kamprad replaced Per Ludvigsson as the chairman of the holding company. Following his decision to step down, the then-87-year-old founder explained, "I see this as a good time for me to leave the board of Inter IKEA Group. By that we are also taking another step in the generation shift that has been ongoing for some years." Mathias and his two older brothers, who also have leadership roles at IKEA, work on the corporation's overall vision and long-term strategy.

Sources of Income

IKEA

IKEA is a multinational group of companies that designs and sells ready-to-assemble furniture (such as beds, chairs and desks), appliances, small motor vehicles and home accessories. As of January 2008, it is the world's largest furniture retailer. Founded in Sweden in 1943 by then-17-year-old Ingvar Kamprad, who was listed as one of the world's richest people in 2013, the company's name is an acronym that consists of the initials of Ingvar Kamprad, Elmtaryd (the farm where he grew up), and Agunnaryd (his hometown in Småland, south Sweden). The company is known for its modern architectural designs for various types of appliances and furniture, and its interior design work is often associated with an eco-friendly simplicity. In addition, the firm is known for its attention to cost control, operational details, and continuous product development, corporate attributes that allowed IKEA to lower its prices by an average of two to three percent over the decade to 2010 during a period of global expansion. The IKEA group has a complex corporate structure

43

and is controlled by several foundations based in the Netherlands, Luxembourg and Liechtenstein.

As of August 2015, IKEA owns and operates 373 stores in 47 countries. In fiscal year 2010, US$23.1 billion worth of goods were sold, a total that represented a 7.7 percent increase over 2009. The IKEA website contains about 12,000 products and is the closest representation of the entire IKEA range. There were over 470 million visitors to IKEA's websites in the year from September 2007 to September 2008. The company is responsible for approximately 1% of world commercial-product wood consumption, making it one of the largest users of wood in the retail sector.

Ingvar Kamprad Quotes

✓ Only those who are asleep make no mistakes.

✓ We ought to have more women in various management positions, because women are the ones who decide almost everything in the home

✓ The most dangerous poison is the feeling of achievement. The antidote is to every evening think what can be done better tomorrow.

✓ Making mistakes is the privilege of the active. It is always the mediocre people who are negative, who spend their time proving that they were not wrong.

✓ The word impossible has been and must remain deleted from our dictionary,

✓ Simplicity and common sense should characterize planning and strategic direction.

✓ Time is your most important resource. You can do so much in ten minutes. Ten minutes; once gone is gone for good.

- ✓ It was our duty to expand. Those who cannot or will not join us are to be pitied. What we want to do, we can do and will do, together. A glorious future!

- ✓ I'm not afraid of turning 80 and I have lots of things to do. I don't have time for dying.

- ✓ Simple routine have a greater impact. It is not just to cut costs that we avoid luxury hotels. We do not need fancy cars, posh titles, tailor made uniforms or other status symbols.

- ✓ Ten minutes are not just one-sixth of your hourly pay; ten minutes is a piece of yourself. Divide yourself into ten units and sacrifice as few of them as possible in meaningless activities. Most things still remain to be done.

- ✓ People say I am cheap, and I don't mind if they do.

- ✓ I could have an office all to myself but since my collaborators don't have one, then I too am contented to have a desk in a shared room.

- ✓ To design a desk which may cost $1,000 is easy for a furniture designer but to design a functional and good desk which shall cost only $50 can only be done by the very best

- ✓ What is good for our customers is also in the long run good for us.

- ✓ How can I ask people who work for me to travel cheaply if I am traveling in luxury?

- ✓ Ikea people do not drive flashy cars or stay at luxury hotels.

- ✓ You can do so much in 10 minutes time. Ten minutes, once gone, are gone for good. Divide your life into 10-minute units and sacrifice as few of them as possible in meaningless activity.

- ✓ We have to still develop the IKEA group. We need many billions of Swiss francs to take on China or Russia.

✓ IKEA is not completely perfect. It irritates me to hear it said that IKEA is the best company in the world. We are going the right way to becoming it but we are not there yet.

✓ A better everyday life means getting away from status and conventions -- being freer and more at ease as human beings.

✓ Everything we earn we need as a reserve.

✓ Waste of resources is a mortal sin at IKEA.

✓ If there is such a thing as good leadership, it is to give a good example. I have to do so for all the Ikea employees.

✓ The IKEA spirit is strong and living reality. Simplicity in our behavior gives us strength. Simplicity and humbleness characterize us in our relations with each others, our suppliers and our customers.

Prince Al-Waleed bin Talal

About

Brief Profile until October 2015

Born	7 March 1955 (age 60)
	Jeddah, Saudi Arabia
Residence	Riyadh, Saudi Arabia
Nationality	Saudi Arabia
	Lebanon
Alma mater	Menlo College
	Syracuse University
Occupation	Chairman & CEO of Kingdom Holding Company
Years active	1979–present
Net worth	US$28 billion (June 2015)
Religion	Islam
Spouse(s)	Dalal bint Saud bin Abdulaziz (divorced)
	Eman bint Naser bin Abdullah al Sudairi (divorced)
	Ameera al-Taweel (divorced)

About Al-Waleed bin Talal

Al-Waleed Bin Talal bin Abdulaziz al Saud (Arabic: بن طلال بن الوليد سعود آل عبدالعزيز, born 7 March 1955) is a Saudi business magnate and investor. He is a member of the Saudi royal family. Waleed was listed as one of Time magazine's Time 100, an annual list of

47

the hundred most influential people in the world in 2008. Waleed is a nephew of the late Saudi King Abdullah, a grandson of Ibn Saud, the first Saudi king, and a grandson of Riad Al Solh, Lebanon's first Prime Minister.

Al-Waleed is the founder, the chief executive officer and 95 percent-owner of the Kingdom Holding Company, a Forbes Global 2000 company with investments in companies within various sectors such as banking and financial services, hotels and hotel management companies, mass media, entertainment, retail, agriculture, petrochemicals, aviation, technology, and real estate. The company has market cap of over $18 billion in 2013. Waleed is also Citigroup's largest individual shareholder, the second-largest voting shareholder in 21st Century Fox, he owns Paris's Four Seasons Hotel George V and part of Plaza Hotel. His business acumen and shrewd entrepreneurial prowess have earned him comparisons to American investor and business magnate Warren Buffett. Due to his prominence as a businessman, he was acknowledged by Time, who labeled the Prince as the "Arabian Warren Buffett". In June 2015 Forbes listed Al-Waleed as the 34th-richest man in the world, with an estimated net worth of US$28 billion.

In 2015 Al-Waleed announced that he would donate his entire fortune to charity at an unspecified date, in order to foster cultural understanding and empower women among other motivations.

Sources of Income

Kingdom Holding Company

The Kingdom Holding Company (Arabic: شركة المملكة القابضة) is an investment holding company based in Riyadh, Saudi Arabia. The Kingdom Holding Company (KHC) is a publicly listed company on the Tadawul (Saudi Stock Exchange). The KHC consists of a select team of experienced investment specialists directed by prince Alwaleed bin Talal. The company describes itself as a diversified investment company, whose main interests are banking / financial services, real estate, hotels, media, entertainment, and Internet / technology.

Its investments include (or have included)

- ✓ 360buy (China / 100%) (present)
- ✓ Amazon (past) (United States - {US})
- ✓ AOL / Time Warner (past) (US)
- ✓ Apple (past) (US)
- ✓ Canary Wharf (UK / now fully American-owned by JP Morgan Chase) (past)
- ✓ Citigroup (present / 2%) (US)
- ✓ Coca-Cola (past) (US)
- ✓ Compaq (past) (US)
- ✓ eBay (past) (US)
- ✓ EuroDisney (past) (France / fully American-owned by the Walt Disney Company)
- ✓ Four Seasons Hotels & Resorts (present / 47.5%) (Canada)
- ✓ Fairmont Hotels and Resorts (present / 1 quarter / shared with the government of Qatar and the American company Colony Capital) (Canada)
- ✓ Ford (past) (US)
- ✓ Hotel George V, Paris (100%) (present) (France)
- ✓ Hewlett-Packard (past) (US)
- ✓ KADCO Egypt (present / 100%) (Egypt)
- ✓ Kingdom Hospital-Consulting Clinics (present) (100% / Saudi Arabia)
- ✓ Kingdom Hotels Investments, (100% / Saudi Arabia) (present)
- ✓ Kingdom Schools (present) (100% / Saudi Arabia)
- ✓ Lebanese Broadcasting Corporation (present) (100% / Lebanon)
- ✓ McDonald's (past) (US)
- ✓ Motorola Mobility (past) (US)
- ✓ Mövenpick Hotels & Resorts (Germany) (present / 33%)
- ✓ Flynas (present / 100% / Saudi Arabia)
- ✓ National Industrialization Company (Saudi Arabia / present / 100%)
- ✓ News Corporation (present / 1%) (US)
- ✓ PepsiCo (past) (US)
- ✓ Priceline.com (past) (US)
- ✓ Procter & Gamble (past) (US)
- ✓ Rotana Group (Arabic: روتانا), the Arab World's largest entertainment company (present / 100%) (Saudi Arabia)
- ✓ Saks Incorporated (past) (US)
- ✓ Savola Group (present) (Saudi Arabia) (100%)

- ✓ SAMBA, Saudi American Bank (past) (US)
- ✓ Saudi Research & Marketing Group (present) (100%) (Saudi Arabia)
- ✓ The Walt Disney Company (past) (US)
- ✓ Twitter (present/2%) (US)

The company is known for hiring the first Saudi female commercial pilot, Captain Hanadi Zakaria al-Hindi, who trained at the Mideast Aviation Academy in Jordan.

It is the owner of and was the lead developer of the Kingdom Centre in Riyadh, Saudi Arabia.

Kingdom Holding is an active investor in sub-saharan Africa through Kingdom Africa Management, a private equity firm and subsidiary based in South Africa, Ghana and Nigeria. Kingdom Africa is run by J. Kofi Bucknor and focuses on growth equity investments.

In 2007, the company committed to purchasing an Airbus A380 "Flying Palace" for $485 million, however according to the Kingdom Holding's chief financial officer the plane has been sold.

In April 2010, the company sold part of its stake in Raffles Holdings International in a deal worth about $847 million. to a group of investors, including an affiliate of Qatar's sovereign wealth fund.

In August 2011, the company announced plans for the construction of Kingdom Tower, which will become the tallest building in the world.

Prince Al-Waleed bin Talal Quotes

- ✓ Actually, King Abdullah, under his supervision and guidance, has established a dialogue in Saudi Arabia whereby all the population, whether Shiite or Sunnis from north, south, west or east, they can get together and exchange their views.

- ✓ I'm telling you, you can't compare Saudi Arabia to other countries.

- ✓ Saudi Arabia has stability. The social contract and the political contract between the king and the rulers and the royal family and the ruled people in Saudi Arabia is very strong and the bondage is so solid.

✓ If I'm going to do something, I do it spectacularly or I don't do it at all.

✓ Most governments are pragmatic, most people are logical. There are pockets of extremism in Israel, in the U.S. and in the Muslim world. But we have to fight them with reason, with logic and with compassion.

✓ No company should depend on one person no matter how that person is smart or genius, whether it's Apple or News Corp, or Citibank or any other company in the world.

✓ I believe Twitter, right now, is just finishing the venture capital phase, getting into a maturity level.

✓ You know, Saudi Arabia has a lot of poverty also. Regardless about what you hear about the viceroy and people being rich, et cetera.

✓ The issue of Palestine has been there since more than 60 years. But more important since 1967 when the war was, ended in the defeat of some Arab countries.

✓ Ethics to me is very important.

✓ I definitely believe that the so-called American decline is greatly exaggerated.

✓ I will always serve my country in any capacity, but I'm very happy with what I'm doing right now.

✓ King Abdullah is a reformer.

✓ Well, clearly Apple is a role model of the American innovation whereby it produced all these products - iPod, iPhone, iPad - that are really now dominating all the technology arena in the world.

51

✓ If the United States has to accept the U.N. resolutions, we have to generalize it across the board. We can't just pick and choose where we impose and accept the U.N. resolution and don't accept them. U.N. Resolution 242 is very clear and states very clearly that Israel has to go back to the borders of the pre-war of 1967.

✓ So, if you look at what's common among some of the companies I have, including the Four Seasons, NewsCorp, George V, the Plaza, these are all irreplaceable brands in their own fields.

✓ We're getting hurt, but I'm a long-term investor.

✓ Those people behind the mosque have to respect, have to appreciate and have to defer to the people of New York. The wound is still there. Just because the wound is healing you can't say, 'Let's just go back to where we were pre-9/11.

✓ Nowadays, anyone who cannot speak English and is incapable of using the Internet is regarded as backward.

✓ Our Palestinian brethren continue to be slaughtered at the hands of Israelis while the world turns the other cheek.

✓ I'm not panicking, and I'm not scared, I've been through the Gulf War, the Asia crisis, and the Russian crisis.

✓ I own almost 100 hotels in North America. Some of them are only in management, but some of them we have some small stakes in them.

✓ My wheels are running. My investments are local, regional and international.

✓ I believe the government of the United States should re-examine its policies in the Middle East and adopt a more balanced stance toward the Palestinian cause.

✓ The lesson is that, No. 1, this management has to be at the highest class possible. No. 2, they have to have a succession plan.

Mukesh Ambani

About

Brief Profile until October 2015

Residence	Mumbai, Maharashtra, India
Nationality	Indian
Ethnicity	Gujarati
Alma mater	Institute of Chemical Technology
	Forest School (Walthamstow)
	Stanford University (discontinued)
Occupation	Chairman of Reliance Industries
Net worth	Decrease US$ 18.9 billion (October 2015)
Religion	Hinduism
Spouse(s)	Nita Ambani
Children	Akash Ambani
Anant Ambani	
Isha Ambani	
Parent(s)	Dhirubhai Ambani
	Kokilaben Ambani

About Mukesh Ambani

Mukesh Dhirubhai Ambani (born 19 April 1957) is an Indian business magnate who is the chairman, managing director and largest shareholder of Reliance Industries Limited (RIL), a Fortune Global 500 company and India's second most valuable company by market value. He resides at the Antilia Building, the world's most expensive property. He holds a 44.7% stake in the company. He is the elder son of the late Dhirubhai Ambani and the brother of Anil Ambani. RIL deals mainly in refining, petrochemicals, and in the oil and gas sectors. Reliance Retail Ltd., another subsidiary, is the largest retailer in India.

In 2014, he was ranked 36 on Forbes list of the world's most powerful people and in 2010, he was included in Forbes's list of "68 people who matter most". As of 2013, he is India's richest man and second richest man in Asia. Ambani retains his title as India's richest person for the ninth consecutive year. Through Reliance, he also owns the Indian Premier League franchise Mumbai Indians. In 2012, Forbes named him one of the richest sports owners in the world.

He has served on the board of directors of Bank of America Corporation and the international advisory board of the Council on Foreign Relations. He was the chairman of the board of Indian Institute of Management Bangalore, which is one of the leading business schools in India.

Sources of Income

Reliance Industries Limited (RIL

Reliance Industries Limited (RIL) is an Indian conglomerate holding company headquartered in Mumbai, Maharashtra, India. Reliance owns businesses across India engaged in energy, petrochemicals, textiles, natural resources, retail and telecommunications. Reliance is the most profitable company in India, the second-largest publicly traded company in India by market capitalization and the second largest company in India as measured by revenue after the government-controlled Indian Oil Corporation. The company is ranked 114th on the Fortune Global 500 list of the world's biggest corporations, as of 2014. RIL contributes approximately 20% of India's total exports.

Mukesh Ambani Quotes

✓ Essentially, whoever is successful, whoever is going to do things that make a difference, is going to be talked about.

- ✓ All of us, in a sense, struggle continuously all the time, because we never get what we want. The important thing which I've really learned is how do you not give up, because you never succeed in the first attempt.

- ✓ My big advantage was to have my father accept me as first-generation.

- ✓ Everybody has equal opportunity, and I think that is true for everything.

- ✓ I don't think that ambition should not be in the dictionary of entrepreneurs. But our ambition should be realistic. You have to realize that you can't do everything.

- ✓ I think that our fundamental belief is that for us growth is a way of life and we have to grow at all times.

- ✓ China and India will, separately and together, unleash an explosion of demand.

- ✓ I personally think that money can do very little. And this has been my experience all across.

- ✓ You have to manage money. Particularly with market economies. You may have a great product, but if your bottom line goes bust, then that's it.

- ✓ The organizational architecture is really that a centipede walks on hundred legs and one or two don't count. So if I lose one or two legs, the process will go on, the organization will go on, the growth will go on.

S. Robson Walton

About

Brief Profile until October 2015

Born	October 28, 1944 (age 70)
	Tulsa, Oklahoma, U.S.
Residence	Bentonville, Arkansas
Education	University of Arkansas
	Columbia Law School
Occupation	Chairman of Walmart
Known for	Walton family fortune
Net worth	Decrease$33.4 billion (July 2015)
Spouse(s)	Melani Lowman-Walton (div.),
	Carolyn Funk (div.),
Parent(s)	Sam Walton (father) (d. 1992)
	Helen Walton (mother) (d. 2007)

About S. Robson Walton

Samuel Robson "Rob" Walton (born October 28, 1944) is an American businessman and is the eldest son of Helen Walton and Sam Walton, founder of Walmart, the world's largest retailer. He is Chairman of the company. In October 2012, Walton was listed as the 11th richest person in the world.

Rob Walton is the eldest child of Sam Walton (d. 1992), cofounder of Wal-Mart, and Helen Walton (d. 2007), with siblings Jim Walton, Alice Walton, and John Walton (d. 2005).

Walton attended The College of Wooster and graduated from the University of Arkansas in 1966 with a bachelor of science degree in business administration, where he was also a member of the Lambda Chi Alpha fraternity. He received a juris doctor degree in 1969 from the Columbia University School of Law. Walton is also a trustee at The College of Wooster.

After graduation Walton became a member of the law firm that represented Wal-Mart, Conner & Winters in Tulsa, Oklahoma. In 1978 he left Tulsa to join Wal-Mart as a senior vice president, and in 1982 he was appointed vice chairman. He was named chairman of the board of directors on April 7, 1992, two days after his father's death.

Along with his siblings, he has pledged about $2 billion to the Walton Family Foundation from 2008 to 2013.

By the time he left Tulsa in 1978, Walton had three children, was divorced from his first wife, and was remarried to Carolyn Funk. He and Carolyn filed for divorce in 2000. He married his third wife Melani Lowman-Walton in 2005.

He is ranked at #17 on the 2013 Forbes list of world billionaires with a net worth of $26.1 billion. On the 2013 Forbes 400 list of the richest people in America he is ranked at #9.

Sources of Income

Walmart

Wal-Mart Stores, Inc., known us Warlart is an American multinational retail corporation that operates a chain of discount department stores and warehouse stores. Headquartered in Bentonville, Arkansas, United States, the company was founded by Sam Walton in 1962 and incorporated on October 31, 1969. It has over 11,000 stores in 28 countries, under a total of 65 banners. The company operates under the Walmart name in the United States and Canada. It operates as Walmart de México y Centroamérica in Mexico, as Asda in the United Kingdom, as Seiyu in Japan, and as Best Price in India. It has wholly owned operations in Argentina, Brazil, and Canada. It also owns and operates the Sam's Club retail warehouses.

Walmart is the world's largest company by revenue, according to the Fortune Global 500 list in 2014, as well as the biggest private employer in the world with 2.2 million employees. Walmart is a family-owned business, as the company is controlled by the Walton family. Sam Walton's heirs own over 50 percent of Walmart through their holding company, Walton Enterprises, and through their individual holdings. It is also one of the world's most valuable companies by market value, and is also the largest grocery retailer in the U.S. In 2009, it generated 51 percent of its US$258 billion (equivalent to $284 billion in 2015) sales in the U.S. from its grocery business.

The company was listed on the New York Stock Exchange in 1972. In the late 1980s and early 1990s, the company rose from a regional to a national giant. By 1988, Walmart was the most profitable retailer in the U.S. and by October 1989, it had become the largest in terms of revenue. Geographically limited to the South and lower Midwest up to the mid 1980s, by the early 1990s the company's presence spanned from coast to coast — Sam's Club opened in New Jersey in November 1989 and the first California outlet opened in Lancaster in July 1990. A Walmart in York, Pennsylvania opened in October 1990, bringing the main store to the Northeast.

Walmart's investments outside North America have seen mixed results: its operations in the United Kingdom, South America, and China are highly successful, whereas ventures in Germany and South Korea failed.

S. Robson Walton Quotes

✓ If you'd rather go to the football game than read a comic, that's fine. I'd rather do both.

✓ I learned from my dad that change and experimentation are constants and important. You have to keep trying new things.

✓ I was small but slow as a college tackle.

✓ Planet Lucy Press? I incorporated myself to deal with publishing and was calling myself Big Bang Incorporated, which of course has to do with the Big Bang at the beginning of creation.

✓ The violence in society, I'm afraid, is perpetrated by the people at the top.

✓ The first thing you need to run for President is a budget of around $20 million dollars a day.

✓ Since the Gulf War, since the new World Order, America is now the number one arms dealer in the world.

✓ Marvel has put out good product. DC has put out good product. Even Image has put out good product, as far as I'm concerned... although it's few and far between. But it's not getting recognized, no matter who's doing it.

✓ Jesus gives his life for the congregation, not the other way around.

✓ It's pretty well known that the CIA has been installing friendly dictators around the world for years.

✓ If you like a story that's totally different and won't know which way it's going... where it's go ing to end up and which way it's going to take you, then I think my work fits the bill.

✓ I went to Vortex and Vortex is a whole 'nother story.

✓ Everything I've done is an old Marvel comic in its' own way.

✓ But basically, I'm trying to write a fun story.

Jim Walton

About

Brief Profile until October 2015

Born	June 7, 1948 (age 67)
	Newport, Arkansas
Residence	Bentonville, Arkansas
Citizenship	United States
Education	Marketing Degree from University of Arkansas - Fayetteville, Arkansas in 1971
Occupation	Chairman of Arvest Bank
	Chairman of Community Publishers
Known for	Walton family fortune
Net worth	DecreaseUS$34.9 billion (July 2015)
Board member of	Arvest Bank
	Community Publishers
	Walmart
Spouse(s)	Lynne McNabb Walton
Children	4
Parent(s)	Sam Walton (father) (d. 1992)
	Helen Walton (mother) (d. 2007)

About Jim Walton

Jim Walton (sometimes James Carr, born June 7, 1948) is the youngest son of Sam Walton, the founder of world's largest retailer Wal-Mart. On the 2015 Forbes list of world billionaires, Jim Walton is ranked at #9 with a net worth of $40.6 billion.

Jim Walton is the third child of Wal-Mart co-founder Sam Walton (d. 1992) and Helen Walton (d. 2007) with siblings Rob Walton, Alice Walton, and John Walton (d. 2005). After graduating from Bentonville High School in 1965 where he was president of his junior class, played football at all-state level and also learned to fly a plane, Walton received a bachelor's degree in Business Administration (BA) Marketing from the University of Arkansas in Fayetteville, Arkansas in 1971, where he was also a member of the Lambda Chi Alpha fraternity. In 1972, he joined Wal-Mart and was involved in its real estate dealings. After serving for four years he moved to the family owned Walton Enterprises as president in 1975.

Jim Walton is the third child of Wal-Mart co-founder Sam Walton (d. 1992) and Helen Walton (d. 2007) with siblings Rob Walton, Alice Walton, and John Walton (d. 2005). After graduating from Bentonville High School in 1965 where he was president of his junior class, played football at all-state level and also learned to fly a plane, Walton received a bachelor's degree in Business Administration (BA) Marketing from the University of Arkansas in Fayetteville, Arkansas in 1971, where he was also a member of the Lambda Chi Alpha fraternity. In 1972, he joined Wal-Mart and was involved in its real estate dealings. After serving for four years he moved to the family owned Walton Enterprises as president in 1975.

On September 28, 2005, Walton replaced his deceased brother, John, on the Wal-Mart Board of Directors. He is currently on the Strategic Planning and Finance committees. He is also CEO of his family owned Arvest Bank and chairman of newspaper firm Community Publishers Inc. (CPI) owned by Jim Walton himself but founded by his father Sam Walton after acquiring the local newspaper the Benton County Daily Record, both operating in Arkansas, Missouri, and Oklahoma. He has pledged about $2 billion to the Walton Family Foundation along with his siblings from 2008 to 2013.

Sources of Income

Walmart

See page 57

Jim Walton Quotes

✓ There is critical mass with high-speed Internet connections, so video is a good user experience. And that means there can be critical mass for advertisers.

Li Ka shing

About

Brief Profile until October 2015

Born	29 July 1928 (age 87)
	Chaozhou, Guangdong, China
Citizenship	Hong Kong, Canada
Education	School drop-out
Occupation	Chairman of Cheung Kong Holdings, Hutchison Whampoa and Li Ka Shing Foundation
Net worth	US$27.8 billion (September 2015)
Religion	Buddhism
Spouse(s)	Chong Yuet Ming (deceased)
Children	Victor Li
	Richard Li

About Li Ka shing

Sir Ka-shing Li, GBM, KBE, JP (born 29 July 1928 in Chaozhou, China) is a Hong Kong business magnate, investor, and philanthropist. According to the Bloomberg Billionaires Index, as of 16 April 2014 he is the richest person in Asia, with a net worth of $31.9 billion. He is the chairman of the board of CK Hutchison Holdings as of 2015; through it, he is the world's largest operator of container terminals and the world's largest health and beauty retailer.

Considered one of the most powerful figures in Asia, Li was named "Asia's Most Powerful Man, Li Ka-Ching" by Asiaweek in 2001. His companies make up 15% of the market capitalisation of the

Hong Kong Stock Exchange. Forbes Magazine and the Forbes family honoured Li Ka-shing with the first ever "Malcolm S. Forbes Lifetime Achievement Award" on 5 September 2006, in Singapore. In spite of his wealth, Li has cultivated a reputation for leading a no-frills lifestyle, and is known to wear simple black dress shoes and an inexpensive Seiko wristwatch. He owns a house in one of Hong Kong's most expensive districts, Deep Water Bay in Hong Kong Island. Li is also regarded as one of Asia's most generous philanthropists, donating over US$2.18 billion as of August 2015 to charity and other various philanthropic causes. Li is often referred to as "Superman" in Hong Kong because of his business prowess. Because of his wealth, he is regarded as a celebrity, and even has a wax statue in his likeness (the only non-artist to have one in Hong Kong).

Li Ka-shing was born in Chaozhou in Guangdong province, China, in 1928 to Teochew people. Due to his father's death, he was forced to leave school before the age of 15 and found a job in a plastics trading company where he worked 16 hours a day. In 1950 he started his own company, Cheung Kong Industries. From manufacturing plastics, Li developed his company into a leading real estate investment company in Hong Kong that was listed on the Hong Kong Stock Exchange in 1972. Cheung Kong expanded by acquiring Hutchison Whampoa and Hongkong Electric Holdings Limited in 1979 and 1985 respectively.

Sources of Income

Cheung Kong Holdings

Cheung Kong (Holdings) Limited, is a multinational conglomerate, based in Hong Kong. It is one of Hong Kong's leading multi-national conglomerates. The company merged with its subsidiary Hutchison Whampoa on 3 June 2015, as part of a major reorganisation, to become part of CK Hutchison Holdings.

The Chairman of Cheung Kong Holdings is Li Ka Shing (李嘉誠), while his elder son, Victor Li, is Managing Director and Deputy Chairman. Li Ka Shing founded Cheung Kong Industries in 1950s as a plastics manufacturer. Under his leadership, the company grew rapidly and eventually evolved into a property investment company. "Cheung Kong (Holdings) Limited" was established in 1971.

The Cheung Kong Group was one of the largest developers of residential, office, retail, industrial and hotel properties in Hong Kong. With its long history of property development expertise and residential estates, Cheung Kong Holdings has built many of Hong Kong's most notable landmark buildings and complexes. As part of the reorganisation of the group, a new company composed of the group's property assets was spun-off in June 2015 as Cheung Kong Property Holdings.

Hutchison Whampoa

Hutchison Whampoa Limited (HWL) is an investment holding company based in Hong Kong. It was a Fortune Global 500 company and one of the largest companies listed on the Hong Kong Stock Exchange. HWL was an international corporation with a diverse array of holdings which included the world's biggest port and telecommunication operations in 14 countries and run under the 3 brand. Its business also included retail, property development and infrastructure. It was 49.97% owned by the Cheung Kong Group.

On 3 June 2015, the company merged with the Cheung Kong Group as part of a major reorganisation of the group's businesses. The combined business was renamed CK Hutchison Holdings Limited.

Originally Hutchison Whampoa was two separate companies, both founded in the 19th century. Hong Kong and Whampoa Dock was established in 1863, by British merchant John Duflon Hutchison, and Hutchison International was formed in 1877.

In the 1960s, Hutchison International – under Colonel Sir Douglas Clague (1917–1981) – gained a controlling interest of Hong Kong and Whampoa Dock, and in 1977 Hutchison acquired all of Hong Kong and Whampoa Dock, creating Hutchison Whampoa Limited.

Although Hutchison Whampoa had a large portfolio of valuable real estate interests, in docks and retail ventures, the company eventually ran into trouble. It was rescued by The Hongkong and

Shanghai Banking Corporation, with HSBC taking a 22% stake in the company and ensuring that Clague was replaced.

On 25 September 1979, at the close of trade in London, HSBC announced that it was selling its stake in Hutchison Whampoa to Cheung Kong for HK$639 million.

In March 2011, Hutchison Port Holdings Trust (HPHT) announced that the company would IPO through Singapore Exchange for about US$5.4 billion. This would be the largest offering in South East Asia and surpass Petronas Chemicals offering of about $4.1 billion.

In January 2015, Li Ka-shing entered into talks with Telefónica to buy its British mobile division O2 for around $15.4 billion. In March 2015, Li Ka-shing confirmed it will be purchasing Telefónica's UK mobile division for £10.25bn subject to regulatory approval by competition regulator, Ofcom.

In January 2015, Li Ka Shing confirmed plans for Cheung Kong Holdings to purchase the remaining shares in Hutchison Whampoa that it did not already own, and merge the two companies as CK Hutchison Holdings. The merger is part of a larger reorganisation of Li's businesses, which will involve the spin-off of property assets into Cheung Kong Property. The new holding company has been incorporated in the Cayman Islands, rather than Hong Kong.

In May 2015, Hutchison revealed plans to sell one-third of its stake in its British-based mobile phone businesses for a potential fee of $4.3 billion to five investors including: GIC Private Limited, Canada Pension Plan Investment Board, Abu Dhabi Investment Authority, BTG Pactual and Caisse de depot et placement du Quebec

Li Ka shing Quotes

✓ Something that seems to be a loss can often turn out to be a gain.

✓ The secret of management is simply identifying and making use of talent.

✓ I wasn't lucky. I worked hard to achieve the goals I set for myself.

✓ The more you know, the more confidence you gain.

✓ First of all, I am an optimist.

✓ Your life is meaningful if you can honestly say that you have done your best to do some good.

✓ When times are tough you need to ask yourself if you're up to it. During tough times I've always thought I'm up to it.

✓ It takes a cool head to do business, as does playing golf. Even if you've teed off badly, as long as you keep your composure, stick to your plan, you may not lose the hole.

✓ Buying land is not like buying antiques, it is not the only deal available.

✓ Be prepared for rainy days. No matter how well you're doing, you've got to be prepared.

✓ In the past years, when the stock market, the property market and the general economy were in the doldrums, we increased our investments. One of the reasons was that we are always prepared. We don't get carried away when times are good and don't get too pessimistic when times are bad.

✓ You give more in order to get more.

✓ If you are good to people, they will be good to you.

✓ Through the years, property is of course the most profitable business. But no line of business remains forever prosperous. At a certain point, there will be market saturation or the government will have new policies. I'd always known this.

✓ Knowledge changes fate.

✓ Money may be spent but never squandered.

✓ Vision is perhaps our greatest strength... it has kept us alive to the power and continuity of thought through the centuries, it makes us peer into the future and lends shape to the unknown.

✓ Information and communications technology unlocks the value of time, allowing and enabling multi-tasking, multi-channels, multi-this and multi-that.

✓ We are approaching a new age of synthesis. Knowledge cannot be merely a degree or a skill... it demands a broader vision, capabilities in critical thinking and logical deduction without which we cannot have constructive progress.

✓ The future may be made up of many factors but where it truly lies is in the hearts and minds of men. Your dedication should not be confined for your own gain, but unleashes your passion for our beloved country as well as for the integrity and humanity of mankind.

✓ I should make more money and use it when opportunity arises. Only making money like this has any meaning.

✓ If you allow your partners to benefit from the deal, they always come back and want to do business with you. There will never be a shortage of opportunity.

✓ It is the man who goes to the table to ask and squeeze for the last nickel who is never happy. Do you know why? It is because that person leaves the table, typically getting the nickel, but then hates himself for not asking for two nickels. As a result, he is never happy.

✓ First of all, I am an optimist. When you study hard and work hard, your knowledge grows, and it gives you confidence. The more you know, the more confidence you gain.

✓ The most important enjoyment for me is to work hard and to make more profit.

✓ People were working eight hours a day, but I worked sixteen hours... It was really full, non-stop work.

✓ During the day I worked in the office to bring in business to sell. After office hours I worked in the factory to see that the orders were taken care of and we'd give good delivery.

✓ In Chinese we have a saying: If you want to be successful, whatever your business or position, you need to accept different opinions and different people.

✓ Why did the Yangtze become a long river? It's because it can accept smaller rivers and become big.

✓ I lived and breathed plastic flowers for ten years, and all day long all I could think of was how to make them look more life-like and how to be more creative.

✓ I firmly believed that property would be one of the best businesses in the future. I could see that the supply of land in Hong Kong was limited, whereas population was unlimited.

✓ I loathe the social scene; I don't like cultivating relationships, and I'm too emotional. These are all weaknesses in doing business.

✓ I also have some strengths. First, I have a thirst for knowledge. Second, I work hard, which can compensate for some of the weaknesses. Most importantly, I know what's right from wrong.

Eike Batista

About

Brief Profile until October 2015

Born	Eike Fuhrken Batista da Silva
	3 November 1956 (age 58)
	Governador Valadares, Minas Gerais, Brazil
Nationality	Brazil
Ethnicity	German Brazilian
	Portuguese Brazilian(Descendant from first Portuguese colonial settlers)
Alma mater	RWTH Aachen University (Dropped out)
Occupation	CEO of EBX Group
Net worth	Increase US$ 200 million (2015)
Spouse(s)	Luma de Oliveira (m. 1991; div. 2004)
Children	Thor Batista (b. 1992)
	Olin Batista (b. 1996)
	Balder Batista (b. 2013)

About Eike Batista

Eike Fuhrken Batista da Silva (born 3 November 1956) is a Brazilian business magnate who made and lost a fortune in mining and oil and gas exploration. Presently, he is the chairman of Brazilian conglomerate EBX Group. The group includes five companies that trade on the BOVESPA's Novo Mercado, a special segment of the São Paulo stock market where enterprises with the highest standards of corporate governance are listed. These five companies are: OGX (oil and gas), MPX (energy), LLX (logistics), MMX (mining) and OSX (offshore services and equipment).

In early 2012, Batista had a net worth of $30.0 billion, making him the seventh wealthiest person in the world and the richest in Brazil. By July 2013, his wealth had plummeted to $200 million due to his debts and company's falling stock prices. Bloomberg reported in January 2014 that Batista "has a negative net worth." Forbes and Folha de S.Paulo quoted Batista in September 2014 stating that his negative net worth was –$1 billion.

Batista is one of seven children of businessman Eliezer Batista da Silva, who was Minister of Mines and Energy in the João Goulart and Fernando Collor administrations and a former president of Companhia Vale do Rio Doce, then wholly a state enterprise, between 1961–1964 and 1979–1986. His mother, Jutta Fuhrken, was born in Germany and, from her, Batista says he learned self-esteem and discipline, attributes he considers crucial to his formation as an entrepreneur. After spending his childhood in Brazil, Batista and his family moved to Europe when he was a teenager, due to his father's occupation. They lived in Geneva, Düsseldorf and Brussels.

In 1974, he began to study metallurgical engineering at the University of Aachen in Germany. When he was 18 years old, his parents returned to Brazil, yet Batista remained abroad and began selling insurance policies door-to-door to make his living. In interviews, he often mentions that the "stress" and the lessons learned from this experience were essential for his education.

Batista-da-Silva returned to Brazil in the early 1980s and focused his attention on the gold and diamond trades. He established himself as a salesman, contacting producers in the Amazon area and buyers in large metropolitan centers in Brazil and Europe. When he was 23 years old, he started a gold trading firm, called Autram Aurem, using the Inca Sun as the company trademark and symbol. A year and a half later, the company had earned US$6 million.

His entrepreneurial instinct and talent led him to implement the first mechanized alluvial gold mining plant in the Amazon, marking the beginning of the EBX Group. At age 29, he became CEO of

TVX Gold, a company listed on the Canadian Stock Exchange, thus initiating his relationship with global capital markets.

From 1980 to 2000, he created US$20 billion in value with the operation of eight gold mines in Brazil and Canada and a silver mine in Chile.

Between 1991 and 1996, the value of his company more than tripled.

Sources of Income

EBX Group

EBX Group comprises six companies listed in BOVESPA's Novo Mercado, the segment that features the highest standards in corporate governance: OGX (oil), MMX (mining), OSX (offshore industry), and CCX (coal mining). These companies are controlled by the Brazilian entrepreneur Eike Batista, the chairman of the EBX Group.

Between 2011 and 2012, EBX Group invested US$ 15.7 billion, generating 20,000 jobs in the construction and operation of its enterprises. Over the succeeding years, it will invest US$ 50 billion. The group has strategic partners and develops projects which focus on state-of-the-art technology and the generation of wealth. EBX primarily invests in the sectors of infrastructure and natural resources. It also has initiatives in real estate, technology, entertainment, sports and gold mining, as well as in the air and rail catering sectors.

EBX Group is active in nine Brazilian states, Chile, Canada and Colombia, and has offices in New York (USA).

Eike Batista Quotes

✓ A brutal desire to be financially independent.

✓ After two and a half years at Aachen University in Germany I realized that I already had a grasp on the engineering part of the world, so I wanted to make money.

- ✓ America and Brazil have allowed the financial people to make money through money. We have forgotten to make things more efficient.

- ✓ Entrepreneurs… need to take a long-term view. Projects that have quality take three to five years to be built.

- ✓ Failures only make you grow.

- ✓ From the 1960s to the 1980s, my father was very busy building the international offices of Vale, the Brazilian steel giant.

- ✓ I always had a great interest in engineering for the sake of making things better.

- ✓ I began selling insurance…This taught me how to talk to people. Some doors open and some do not.

- ✓ I had to airlift the gold out. The closest road was 100 kilometers from the mine…

- ✓ I learned to think.

- ✓ I like a challenge.

- ✓ I made $6 million when I was twenty-two years of age.

- ✓ I owned a motorbike that went 90 to 100 kilometers an hour. I spent hours trying to make it faster.

- ✓ I see myself as an entrepreneur. Somehow I have a pact with Mother Nature. I drill and I find things. Somehow you have to have luck.

- ✓ I simply didn't want to get money from my parents anymore. This was very powerful.

- ✓ I tell young people, especially middle and upper-class youngsters, that parents should not make it too easy for them. We pamper them too much.

- ✓ I want to be the world's biggest philanthropist.

✓ I was down to my last $300,000 because I had obviously under-estimated logistics, diseases, and mechanical problems... It was very stressful, I must tell you.

✓ I went to two jewelers in Rio and asked them to lend me some money. I said I would bring the gold to Rio and Sao Paulo from the Amazon. Somehow, they liked what I said and obviously it was gold, you know. I don't think they would have given me any money if I asked them to buy chocolate.

✓ I went to visit the Amazon in the northern part of Brazil, where lots of pick-and-shovel miners were producing lots of gold. It was like the old Wild West.

✓ I'm one of seven children, the second.

✓ I'm very competitive.

✓ I've made it a mission to help a new generation of Brazilian entrepreneurs be successful in a more transparent way. They should be proud of what they are creating.

✓ If you look at the world through the eyes of an engineer, there are a lot of opportunities.

✓ In 1989, when I decided to race powerboats in Brazil, I became the Brazilian, the American and the world champion because of two things: understanding how to build a team and smart engineering. It's a very dangerous sport and a five-cent piece could make you lose the race or even die.

✓ In mining you go to some crazy place, you set up a camp. You start looking for water and energy and this way you can build anything. That's the mind-set. That's my life. That's how I started from zero.

✓ My advice to young people is start small and think long term.

✓ My mother taught me discipline – she was German, from Hamburg – and so she taught me discipline and care, caring for others, which is very much what I got from her, which forged me in many ways.

✓ Somehow I have a pact with nature. Everywhere I drill I find oil, coal or gold.

✓ The mine was so rich it was totally idiot-proof.

✓ Wealth creation is all about in natural resources, is identifying seeing these things and putting the right people together to make it happen, produce it.

✓ What I have learned in the 30 years is to - I read people better than I read books.

✓ What I realized was that a lot of gold was being produced and so my idea was to become a trader, to buy and sell the gold. I didn't want to initially participate in the gold production because local owners who had the planes and controlled the landing strips to move the gold out controlled it. The mules of the jungle were Cessna 186 planes.

✓ What my father taught me, what I learned from him, is to think big, because he built – there's a movie in Brazil called Brazil's Engineer, and it's about him, because he built part of Brazil's macro-infrastructure – railways, super ports for shipment of iron ore to Asia, back then to Japan. And so I learned to think.

✓ When I was eleven or twelve I had asthma. My mother said I think you could cure this through swimming. And she kept throwing me into a swimming pool to the point that I solved my asthma problem. That was added stress in my life, and it makes you tougher.

John Walton

About

Brief Profile until October 2015

Born	John Thomas Walton
	October 18, 1946
	Newport, Arkansas, U.S.
Died	June 27, 2005 (aged 58)Jackson, Wyoming, U.S.
Cause of death	Plane crash
Resting place	Bentonville Cemetery,
	Bentonville, Arkansas, U.S.
Spouse(s)	Mary Ann Gunn (divorced)
	Christy Walton, 1 child
Children	Lukas (son)

About John Walton

John Thomas Walton (October 8, 1946 – June 27, 2005) was a United States war veteran and a son of Walmart founder Sam Walton. He was also the chairman of True North Partners, a venture capital firm. Walton cofounded the Children's Scholarship Fund, providing tuition scholarships for disadvantaged youth.

Walton graduated from Bentonville High School where he was a star football player. Walton went on to attend the College of Wooster in Wooster, Ohio. He dropped out of college in 1968 to spend more time playing the flute and enlisted in the U.S. Army (after the Vietnamese Tet Offensive).

During the Vietnam war Walton served in the Green Berets as part of the Studies and Observations Group. He was involved in combat in the A Shau Valley and in Laos, where he was the medic and second-in-command of a unit named "Spike Team Louisiana". Walton later received a Silver Star for bravery in combat.

After returning from Vietnam Walton learned to fly and went to work as a pilot for Wal-Mart. He later left the company to fly crop-dusters over cotton fields in several southern states and co-founded Satloc, an aerial application company that pioneered the use of GPS technology in agricultural crop-dusting. Walton then moved to San Diego where he founded Corsair Marine, a company that built trimaran sailboats. He also lived in Durango, Colorado, and was an enthusiastic skier, mountain biker, hiker, motorcycle rider, sky diver and scuba diver.

In 1998, as part of the Philanthropy Roundtable, Walton and friend Ted Forstmann established the Children's Scholarship Fund to provide tuition assistance for low-income families to send their children to private schools. He was an advocate of school vouchers. For his achievements, he received the William E. Simon Prize for Philanthropic Leadership.

Sources of Income

Walmart

See page 57

John Walton Quotes

- ✓ I figured if you're going to do something, you should do it the best you can.

- ✓ There is a growing acceptance and interest in publicly funded school choice as a catalyst for education reform in general and a way to empower parents to be education reformers.

Alice Walton

About

Brief Profile until October 2015

Born	Alice Louise Walton
	October 7, 1949 (age 66)
	Newport, Arkansas, US
Residence	Millsap, Texas, US
Citizenship	United States
Education	Trinity University
Known for	Heiress, Walton family fortune
Net worth	DecreaseUS$33.7 billion (July 2015)
Board member of	Amon Carter Museum
Spouse(s)	Divorced
Parent(s)	Sam Walton, Helen Walton

About Alice Walton

Alice Louise Walton (born October 7, 1949) is an American heiress to the fortune of Wal-Mart Stores, Inc. She is the daughter of Wal-Mart founder Sam Walton and Helen Walton, and sister of the late John T. Walton, S. Robson Walton and Jim Walton. Her estimated net worth is US$34.3 billion, making her the second richest woman in the world (behind Liliane Bettencourt and ahead of her sister-in-law Christy Walton). As of February 2014, according to the Bloomberg Billionaires Index her estimated net worth was US$33.9 billion, making her the 13th richest person in the world. The Hurun Report Global Rich List, published in February 2014, ranks her as second-richest woman in the world. She has been arrested multiple times for driving while intoxicated, and in 1989, she was involved in the speeding death of a 50-year-old woman, Oleta Hardin, a cannery worker, but no charges were filed.

Walton was born in Newport, Arkansas. She graduated from Trinity University in San Antonio, Texas, with a B.A. in economics and finance. She began her career in finance as an equity analyst and money manager for First Commerce Corporation and later served as vice chairperson and head of all investment-related activities at the Arvest Bank Group. In 1988, Walton founded Llama Company, an investment bank engaged in corporate finance, public and structured finance, real estate finance and sales and trading. She served as President, Chairperson and CEO. For a time, she was a broker for E.F. Hutton.

She was the first chairperson and driving force behind the Northwest Arkansas Council. This community development organization played a major role in securing the development of the Northwest Arkansas Regional Airport. In the late 1990s, Walton closed Llama Company and moved to a 3,200-acre (1,300 ha) ranch in Millsap, Texas, named Walton's Rocking W Ranch. An avid horse-lover, Walton currently lives in a sprawling one-story, 4,432-square-foot (411.7 m2), stucco house on the horse ranch. She is known for having an eye for determining which 2-month-olds will grow to be champion cutters.

Walton arranged for and provided the initial seed capital to finance the construction of the airport. Her involvement was instrumental in the creation of the airport, and in recognition of her contribution to the airport project and her support of transportation improvements throughout the region, the Airport Authority Board of Directors named the airport terminal the Alice L. Walton Terminal Building. In 2001, Walton was inducted into the Arkansas Aviation Hall of Fame.

Sources of Income

Walmart

See Page 57

Alice Walton Quotes

✓ One of the great responsibilities that I have is to manage my assets wisely, so that they create value.

✓ There is a lot that horses and art share in common. I have found that most horse people are art lovers, and vice versa.

✓ I know the price of lettuce. You need to understand price and value. You buy the best lettuce you can at the best price you can.

✓ I think it is more of an intuitive, circular kind of personality, for starters. And, as I say of horses, the secret to breeding great horses is the three B's: bones, brains, and balance. If you look at art, it shares some of the same qualities.

Helen Walton

About

Brief Profile until October 2015

Born	Helen Robson Kemper
	December 3, 1919
	Claremore, Oklahoma, U.S.
Died	April 19, 2007 (aged 87)
	Bentonville, Arkansas, U.S.
Alma mater	University of Oklahoma
Known for	Walton family fortune
Net worth	Increase US $16.4 billion (est.)
	(March 2007)
Spouse(s)	Sam Walton (1943–1992, his death)

About Helen Walton

Helen Robson Kemper Walton (December 3, 1919 – April 19, 2007) was the wife of Wal-Mart and Sam's Club founder Sam Walton. At one point in her life, she was the richest American and the eleventh-richest woman in the world.

Helen was the valedictorian of her high school class in Claremore, Oklahoma, and a graduate of the University of Oklahoma at Norman with a degree in business. She was the daughter of L.S. Robson, a prosperous rancher. She married Sam Walton on Valentine's Day, February 14, 1943.

Helen and Sam Walton had four children: sons Samuel Robson (Rob) (born 1944), John Thomas (1946-2005), James Carr (Jim) (born 1948), and daughter Alice Louise (born 1949).

When Sam Walton died in 1992, he left his ownership in Wal-Mart to Helen and their four children.

In the last eight years of her life, Helen suffered from dementia but gained peace painting watercolors. "They're abstract but just lyrical and beautiful," said her daughter Alice in an October 2013 interview with Forbes. "I have two. One's very happy and...oh, whimsical, I guess you would say. Then there's one she did right before she died. I mean, you could almost tell. She knew."

She died of heart failure on April 19, 2007. At the time of her death, she had an estimated net worth of $16.4 billion. Ms. Walton was survived by her brother, Frank Robson; three children, S. Robson Walton, Jim C. Walton, and Alice L. Walton; eight grandchildren; and four great-grandchildren.

Sources of Income

Walmart

See page 57

Helen Walton Quotes

✓ It is not what you gather but what you scatter that tells what kind of life you have lived.

Charles Koch

About

Brief Profile until October 2015

Born	Charles de Ganahl Koch
	November 1, 1935 (age 79)
	Wichita, Kansas, US
Residence	Wichita, Kansas, US
Alma mater	Massachusetts Institute of Technology (B.S., M.S.)
Occupation	Chairman and CEO of Koch Industries
Net worth	US$ 41.2 billion (June 2015)
Children	Chase Koch
	Elizabeth Koch
Parent(s)	Mary Robinson
	Fred C. Koch

About Charles Koch

Charles de Ganahl Koch (born November 1, 1935) is an American businessman and philanthropist. He is co-owner, chairman of the board, and chief executive officer of Koch Industries, while his brother David H. Koch serves as Executive Vice President. Charles and David each own 42% of the conglomerate. The brothers inherited the business from their father, Fred C. Koch, then expanded the business. Originally involved exclusively in oil refining and chemicals, Koch Industries now includes process and pollution control equipment and technologies; polymers and fibers; minerals; fertilizers; commodity trading and services; forest and consumer products; and ranching. The businesses produce a wide variety of well-known brands, such as Stainmaster carpet, the Lycra brand of spandex fiber, Quilted Northern tissue and Dixie Cup.

In 2007, Koch's book The Science of Success was published. The book describes his management philosophy, referred to as "Market-Based Management".

Koch Industries is the second-largest privately held company by revenue in the United States according to a 2010 Forbes survey In February 2014, Koch was ranked 9th richest person in the world by Hurun Report with an estimated net worth of $36 billion. Previously, in October 2012 he was ranked the 6th richest person in the world with an estimated net worth of $34 billion—according to the Bloomberg Billionaires Index—and was ranked 18th on Forbes World's Billionaires list of 2011 (and 4th on the Forbes 400), with an estimated net worth of $25 billion, deriving from his 42% stake in Koch Industries.

Koch supports a number of free market-oriented educational organizations, including the Institute for Humane Studies and the Mercatus Center at George Mason University. He also contributes to the Republican Party and candidates, Libertarian groups, and various charitable and cultural institutions. He co-founded the Washington, DC-based Cato Institute. Through the Koch Cultural Trust, founded by Charles Koch's wife, Elizabeth, the Koch family has also funded artistic projects and creative artists.

Sources of Income

Koch Industries

Koch Industries, Inc. is an American multinational corporation based in Wichita, Kansas, United States, with subsidiaries involved in manufacturing, trading, and investments. It was founded as Wood River Oil and Refining Company in 1940, and later as Rock Island Oil & Refining Company.

Koch also owns Invista, Georgia-Pacific, Molex, Flint Hills Resources, Koch Pipeline, Koch Fertilizer, Koch Minerals, and Matador Cattle Company. Koch companies are involved in core industries such as the manufacturing, refining, and distribution of petroleum, chemicals, energy, fiber, intermediates and polymers, minerals, fertilizers, pulp and paper, chemical technology equipment, ranching, finance, commodities trading, and other ventures and investments. The firm employs about 60,000 people in the United States and another 40,000 in 59 other countries.

In 2013, Forbes called it the second largest privately held company in the United States (after Cargill), with an annual revenue of $115 billion, down from the largest in 2006. If Koch Industries were a public company in 2013, it would have ranked 17 in the Fortune 500.

Fred C. Koch, after whom Koch Industries, Inc. is named, co-founded the company in 1940 and developed an innovative crude oil refining process. His sons, Charles Koch, chairman of the board and chief executive officer, and David H. Koch, executive vice president, are principal owners of the company after they bought out their brothers, Frederick and William "Bill" Koch, for $1.1 billion in 1983. Charles and David H. Koch each own 42% of Koch Industries. Charles has stated that the company would go public "over my dead body".

Charles Koch Quotes

✓ Allowing people the freedom to pursue their own interests, within beneficial rules of just conduct, is the best and only sustainable way to promote societal progress.

✓ Businesses' visions must – and do – change.

✓ By instilling a work ethic in me at an early age, my father did me a big favor, although it didn't seem like a favor back then. By the time I was eight, he made sure work occupied most of my spare time.

✓ Creating superior value means generating greater value from the resources consumed than alternate uses.

✓ Do what you have a passion for and is most rewarding to you.

✓ Embrace change. Envision what could be, challenge the status quo, and drive creative destruction.

✓ For business to survive and prosper, it must create real long-term value in society through principled behavior.

✓ I am convinced the combination of our market based philosophy and how we practice it has been the primary source of our success.

✓ I developed two strong passions. The first was to help build a great company. The second was to identify and understand the principles that lead to prosperity and societal progress. After studying history, economics, philosophy, science psychology and other disciplines, I concluded that the two passions were strongly, indeed intimately related.

✓ I understood the natural world operated according to fixed laws... I came to realize that there were, likewise, laws that govern human well-being.

✓ In a return free market, with beneficial rules and property rights, the appropriate measure of the enterprise's value creation is long-term profitability.

✓ It prompted my father to advise me to 'never sue; the lawyers get a third, the government gets a third and you get your business destroyed.' I've tried to follow his advice and have filed very few lawsuits. Unfortunately, he forgot to tell me how to keep from being sued.

✓ Just as central planning is a failure in running government, so it is at the level of the firm.

✓ My father stressed the importance of humility as well as hard work. When I arrived in Wichita, his first words to me were: 'I hope your first deal is a loser, otherwise you will think you're a lot smarter than you are.' He had nothing to worry about – I got us in plenty of losers.

✓ My father, Fred C Koch, born in 1900, saw little future in Quanah or the printing business. He left to study engineering...

- ✓ My father, who co-founded the company that would become Koch Industries. He exemplified much of what is centrally important to us: the value of hard work, integrity, humility and a lifelong dedication to learning.

- ✓ Our willingness to move quickly, absorb more risk and give better service enabled us to become the leading crude oil gathering company.

- ✓ Past performance does not guarantee future success.

- ✓ People benefit through profit and loss according to the value they create in society.

- ✓ Prosperity is only possible in a system where property rights are clearly and properly defined and protected, people are free to speak, exchange and contract, and prices are free to guide beneficial action.

- ✓ Prudent risk-taking should be encouraged by applying the concept of opportunity cost.

- ✓ Successful entrepreneurs are not deterred by their lack of authority to control resources.

- ✓ Surprisingly, my father gave me almost complete freedom in the management of Koch Engineering. He told me I could do anything I wanted with it, short of selling it.

- ✓ The most difficult and painful of all changes: A change in the way we think.

- ✓ The process of discovery begins when we observe, often vaguely, a gap between what is and what could be.

- ✓ To the person with only a hammer and no understanding, every problem looks like a nail.

- ✓ True failures, are lost opportunities, the things you should have done but didn't.

✓ Vision for us is not a one-time statement of goals and aspirations, but a dynamic concept, always evolving based on continual examination of how we can create value for our customers and for society.

✓ We all tend to pursue our own interests, but in a true market economy we can only prosper by providing others with what they value.

✓ We don't enter into partnerships without an exit mechanism.

✓ We must measure what leads to results, not simply what is easy to measure.

✓ When everyone gets something for nothing, soon no one will have anything, because no one will be producing anything.

✓ You've go to be honest with people. You've got to challenge. You've go to give people honest feedback .

David Koch

About

Brief Profile until October 2015

Born	David Hamilton Koch
	May 3, 1940 (age 75)
	Wichita, Kansas, USA
Monuments	David H. Koch Theater
Residence	Manhattan, New York, United States
Citizenship	American
Education	M.S. in Chemical Engineering
Alma mater	Massachusetts Institute of Technology (B.S., M.S.)
Occupation	VP of Koch Industries
Known for	Philanthropy to cultural and medical institutions;
	Support of libertarian and conservative causes
Net worth	US$ 41.2 billion (June 2015)
Board member of	Aspen Institute, Cato Institute, Reason Foundation, Americans for Prosperity Foundation, WGBH, Massachusetts Institute of Technology, Americans for Prosperity, Smithsonian National Museum of Natural History, Metropolitan Museum of Art, American Ballet Theatre, Lincoln Center for the Performing Arts, Deerfield Academy, New York-

Presbyterian Hospital, Memorial Sloan-Kettering Cancer Center, American Museum of Natural History

Spouse(s)   Julia M. Flesher Koch

Children   David Koch Jr.

                     Mary Julia Koch

                     John Mark Koch

Parent(s)   Fred Koch

                     Mary Robinson

About David Koch

David Hamilton Koch (/ˈkoʊk/; born May 3, 1940) is an American businessman, philanthropist, political activist, and chemical engineer. He joined the family business Koch Industries, a conglomerate that is the second-largest privately held company in the United States, in 1970. He became president of the subsidiary Koch Engineering in 1979, and became a co-owner of Koch Industries, with older brother Charles, in 1983. He is now an executive vice president.

Koch is an influential libertarian. He was the 1980 candidate for Vice President of the United States from the United States Libertarian Party and helped finance the campaign. He founded Citizens for a Sound Economy. He and his brother Charles have donated to political advocacy groups and to political campaigns, almost entirely Republican.

Condé Nast Portfolio described him as "one of the most generous but low-key philanthropists in America". Koch has contributed to several charities including Lincoln Center, Sloan Kettering, a fertility clinic at New York-Presbyterian Hospital and the American Museum of Natural History's David H. Koch Dinosaur Wing. The New York State Theater at Lincoln Center, home of the New York City Ballet was renamed the David H. Koch Theater in 2008 following a gift of 100 million dollars for the renovation of the theater.

Koch is the fourth richest person in America as of 2012, and the wealthiest resident of New York City as of 2013. He is the ninth-wealthiest person in the world, as of 2014.

He is a survivor of the USAir Flight 1493 crash in 1991.

Sources of Income

Koch Industries

See page 84

David Koch Quotes

- ✓ 'The Nutcracker' is the ballet that keeps on giving.

- ✓ When I was a bachelor with a different girl on my arm every week, people didn't think I was quite legitimate.

- ✓ The way I look at it is, cancer research is absolutely nonpartisan. Cancer is very democratic in the sense that it attacks people regardless of their race, their gender, their national background, or their political persuasions.

- ✓ You know, once you've stood up to cancer, everything else feels like a pretty easy fight.

- ✓ I think to balance the budget, probably every federal department has to take cuts in my opinion.

- ✓ The only dancing I did was at the discotheques. I was a very good disco dancer. I say that I learned disco dancing at the wrong places.

- ✓ When our bodies are violated by this horrible disease of cancer, we're in total shock because it's so unexpected.

- ✓ I went to my first dinosaur hall with my father and twin brother. We went to the American Museum of Natural History, and I was blown away by the dinosaurs.

- ✓ I was gaga about dinosaurs as a kid.

Part Two

In this part you will see list of richest people of the twenty first century to date (2000 – 2014).

You will first see the list of richest people for the whole period and also you will see each year's list from 2000 to 2014.

Top twenty 2000 – 2014

Name	Rank	Wealth USD Bil'	Source(s) of wealth
Bill Gates United States	1	76.0	Microsoft
Warren Buffett United States	2	62.0	Berkshire Hathaway
Carlos Slim Mexico	3	73.0	Telmex, América Móvil, Grupo Carso
Larry Ellison United States	4	47.0	Oracle Corporation
Amancio Ortega Spain	5	64.0	Inditex Group
Lakshmi Mittal India	6	25.0	Mittal Steel Company
Bernard Arnault France	7	41.0	LVMH Moët Hennessy • Louis Vuitton
Karl Albrecht Germany	8	23.0	Aldi Süd
Paul Allen United States	9	30.4	Microsoft
Ingvar Kamprad Sweden	10	33.0	IKEA
Prince Al-Waleed Saudi Arabia	11	21.5	Kingdom Holding Company
Mukesh Ambani India	12	29.0	Reliance Industries
S. Robson Walton United States	13	20.0	Wal-Mart
Jim Walton United States	14	20.8	Wal-Mart
Li Ka shing Hong Kong, Canada	15	31.0	Cheung Kong Holdings
Karl and Theo Albrecht Germany	16	25.6	Aldi Süd
Eike Batista Brazil	17	30.0	EBX Group
John Walton	18	20.7	Wal-Mart

United States			
Alice Walton **United States**	19	20.0	Wal-Mart
Helen Walton **United States**	20	20.0	Wal-Mart

Top ten 2000

Name	This Year Rank	Over All Rank	Wealth USD Bil'	Source(S) Of Wealth
Bill Gates United States	1	1	60.0	Microsoft
Larry Ellison United States	2	4	47.0	Oracle Corporation
Paul Allen United States	3	9	28.0	Microsoft
Warren Buffett United States	4	2	25.6	Berkshire Hathaway
Karl and Theo Albrecht Germany	5	16	20.0	Aldi Süd
Prince Al-Waleed Saudi Arabia	6	11	20.0	Kingdom Holding Company
S. Robson Walton United States	7	13	20.0	Wal-Mart
Masayoshi Son Japan	8	33	19.4	Softbank Capital, SoftBank Mobile
Michael Dell United States	9	34	19.1	Dell
Kenneth Thomson Canada	10	27	16.1	The Thomson Corporation

Top ten 2001

Name	This Year Rank	Over All Rank	Wealth USD Bil'	Source(S) Of Wealth
Bill Gates United States	1	1	58.7	Microsoft
Warren Buffett United States	2	2	32.3	Berkshire Hathaway
Paul Allen United States	3	9	30.4	Microsoft
Larry Ellison United States	4	4	26.0	Oracle Corporation
Karl and Theo Albrecht Germany	5	16	25.0	Aldi Süd
Prince Al-Waleed Saudi Arabia	6	11	20.0	Kingdom Holding Company
Jim Walton United States	7	14	18.8	Wal-Mart
John Walton United States	8	18	18.7	Wal-Mart
S. Robson Walton United States	9	13	18.6	Wal-Mart
Alice Walton United States	10	19	18.5	Wal-Mart
Helen Walton United States	10	20	18.5	Wal-Mart

Top ten 2002

Name	This Year Rank	Over All Rank	Wealth USD Bil'	Source(S) Of Wealth
Bill Gates **United States**	1	1	52.8	Microsoft
Warren Buffett **United States**	2	2	35.0	Berkshire Hathaway
Karl and Theo Albrecht **Germany**	3	16	26.8	Aldi Süd
Paul Allen **United States**	4	9	25.2	Microsoft
Larry Ellison **United States**	5	4	23.5	Oracle Corporation
Jim Walton **United States**	6	14	20.8	Wal-Mart
John Walton **United States**	7	18	20.7	Wal-Mart
Alice Walton **United States**	8	19	20.5	Wal-Mart
S. Robson Walton **United States**	9	13	20.5	Wal-Mart
Helen Walton **United States**	10	20	20.4	Wal-Mart

Top ten 2003

Name	This Year Rank	Over All Rank	Wealth USD Bil'	Source(S) Of Wealth
Bill Gates **United States**	1	1	40.7	Microsoft
Warren Buffett **United States**	2	2	30.5	Berkshire Hathaway
Karl and Theo Albrecht **Germany**	3	16	25.6	Aldi Süd
Paul Allen **United States**	4	9	20.1	Microsoft
Prince Al-Waleed **Saudi Arabia**	5	11	17.7	Kingdom Holding Company
Larry Ellison **United States**	6	4	16.6	Oracle Corporation
Alice Walton **United States**	7	19	16.5	Wal-Mart
Helen Walton **United States**	8	20	16.5	Wal-Mart
Jim Walton **United States**	9	14	16.5	Wal-Mart
S. Robson Walton **United States**	10	13	16.5	Wal-Mart
John Walton **United States**	10	18	16.5	Wal-Mart

Top ten 2004

Name	This Year Rank	Over All Rank	Wealth USD Bil'	Source(S) Of Wealth
Bill Gates **United States**	1	1	46.6	Microsoft
Warren Buffett **United States**	2	2	42.9	Berkshire Hathaway
Karl Albrecht **Germany**	3	8	23.0	Aldi Süd
Prince Al-Waleed **Saudi Arabia**	4	11	21.5	Kingdom Holding Company
Paul Allen **United States**	5	9	21.0	Microsoft
Alice Walton **United States**	6	19	20.0	Wal-Mart
Helen Walton **United States**	7	20	20.0	Wal-Mart
Jim Walton **United States**	8	14	20.0	Wal-Mart
John Walton **United States**	9	18	20.0	Wal-Mart
S. Robson Walton **United States**	10	13	20.0	Wal-Mart

Top ten 2005

Name	This Year Rank	Over All Rank	Wealth USD Bil'	Source(S) Of Wealth
Bill Gates **United States**	1	1	46.5	Microsoft
Warren Buffett **United States**	2	2	44.0	Berkshire Hathaway
Lakshmi Mittal **India**	3	6	25.0	Mittal Steel Company
Carlos Slim **Mexico**	4	3	23.8	Telmex
Prince Al-Waleed **Saudi Arabia**	5	11	23.7	Kingdom Holding Company
Ingvar Kamprad **Sweden**	6	10	23.0	IKEA
Paul Allen **United States**	7	9	21.0	Microsoft
Karl Albrecht **Germany**	8	8	18.5	Aldi Süd
Larry Ellison **United States**	9	4	18.4	Oracle Corporation
S. Robson Walton **United States**	10	13	18.3	Walmart

Top ten 2006

Name	This Year Rank	Over All Rank	Wealth USD Bil'	Source(S) Of Wealth
Bill Gates **United States**	1	1	52.0	Microsoft
Warren Buffett **United States**	2	2	42.0	Berkshire Hathaway
Carlos Slim **Mexico**	3	3	30.0	Telmex
Ingvar Kamprad **Sweden**	4	10	28.0	IKEA
Lakshmi Mittal **India**	5	6	23.5	Mittal Steel Company
Paul Allen **United States**	6	9	22.0	Microsoft
Bernard Arnault **France**	7	7	21.5	LVMH Moët Hennessy • Louis Vuitton
Prince Al-Waleed **Saudi Arabia**	8	11	20.0	Kingdom Holding Company
Kenneth Thomson **Canada**	9	27	19.6	The Thomson Corporation
Li Ka Shing **Hong Kong, Canada**	10	15	18.8	Cheung Kong Group, Hutchison Whampoa

Top ten 2007

Name	This Year Rank	Over All Rank	Wealth USD Bil'	Source(S) Of Wealth
Bill Gates United States	1	1	56.0	Microsoft
Warren Buffett United States	2	2	52.0	Berkshire Hathaway
Carlos Slim Mexico	3	3	49.0	Telmex, América Móvil, Grupo Carso
Ingvar Kamprad Sweden	4	10	33.0	IKEA
Lakshmi Mittal India	5	6	32.0	Arcelor Mittal
Sheldon Adelson United States	6	23	26.5	Las Vegas Sands
Bernard Arnault France	7	7	26.0	LVMH
Amancio Ortega Spain	8	5	24.0	Inditex Group
Li Ka shing Hong Kong, Canada	9	15	23.0	Cheung Kong Holdings, Hutchison Whampoa
David Thomson Canada	10	32	22.0	Thomson Corporation

Top ten 2008

Name	This Year Rank	Over All Rank	Wealth USD Bil'	Source(S) Of Wealth
Warren Buffett **United States**	1	2	62.0	Berkshire Hathaway
Carlos Slim **Mexico**	2	3	60.0	Telmex, América Móvil
Bill Gates **United States**	3	1	58.0	Microsoft
Lakshmi Mittal **India**	4	6	45.0	Arcelor Mittal
Mukesh Ambani **India**	5	12	43.0	Reliance Industries
Anil Ambani **India**	6	26	42.0	Anil Dhirubhai Ambani Group
Ingvar Kamprad **Sweden**	7	10	31.0	IKEA
Kushal Pal Singh **India**	8	28	30.0	DLF Group
Oleg Deripaska **Russia**	9	30	28.0	Rusal
Karl Albrecht **Germany**	10	8	18.3	Aldi Süd

Top ten 2009

Name	This Year Rank	Over All Rank	Wealth USD Bil'	Source(S) Of Wealth
Bill Gates United States	1	1	40.0	Microsoft
Warren Buffett United States	2	2	37.0	Berkshire Hathaway
Carlos Slim Mexico	3	3	35.0	Telmex, América Móvil
Larry Ellison United States	4	4	22.5	Oracle Corporation
Ingvar Kamprad Sweden	5	10	22.0	IKEA
Karl Albrecht Germany	6	8	21.5	Aldi Süd
Mukesh Ambani India	7	12	19.5	Reliance Industries
Lakshmi Mittal India	8	6	19.3	Arcelor Mittal
Theo Albrecht Germany	9	25	18.8	Aldi Nord, Trader Joe's
Amancio Ortega Spain	10	5	18.3	Inditex Group

Top ten 2010

Name	This Year Rank	Over All Rank	Wealth USD Bil'	Source(S) Of Wealth
Carlos Slim **Mexico**	1	3	53.5	Telmex, América Móvil, Grupo Carso
Bill Gates **United States**	2	1	53.0	Microsoft
Warren Buffett **United States**	3	2	47.0	Berkshire Hathaway
Mukesh Ambani **India**	4	12	29.0	Reliance Industries
Lakshmi Mittal **India**	5	6	28.7	Arcelor Mittal
Larry Ellison **United States**	6	4	28.0	Oracle Corporation
Bernard Arnault **France**	7	7	27.5	LVMH Moët Hennessy • Louis Vuitton
Eike Batista **Brazil**	8	17	27.0	EBX Group
Amancio Ortega **Spain**	9	5	25.0	Inditex Group
Karl Albrecht **Germany**	10	8	23.5	Aldi Süd

Top ten 2011

Name	This Year Rank	Over All Rank	Wealth USD Bil'	Source(S) Of Wealth
Carlos Slim Mexico	1	3	74.0	Telmex, América Móvil, Grupo Carso
Bill Gates United States	2	1	56.0	Microsoft
Warren Buffett United States	3	2	50.0	Berkshire Hathaway
Bernard Arnault France	4	7	41.0	LVMH Moët Hennessy • Louis Vuitton
Larry Ellison United States	5	4	39.5	Oracle Corporation
Lakshmi Mittal India	6	6	31.1	Arcelor Mittal
Amancio Ortega Spain	7	5	31.0	Inditex Group
Eike Batista Brazil	8	17	30.0	EBX Group
Mukesh Ambani India	9	12	27.0	Reliance Industries
Christy Walton & family United States	10	24	26.5	Walmart

Top ten 2012

Name	This Year Rank	Over All Rank	Wealth USD Bil'	Source(S) Of Wealth
Carlos Slim **Mexico**	1	3	69.0	Telmex, América Móvil, Grupo Carso
Bill Gates **United States**	2	1	61.0	Microsoft
Warren Buffett **United States**	3	2	44.0	Berkshire Hathaway
Bernard Arnault **France**	4	7	41.0	LVMH Moët Hennessy • Louis Vuitton
Amancio Ortega **Spain**	5	5	37.5	Inditex Group
Larry Ellison **United States**	6	4	36.0	Oracle Corporation
Eike Batista **Brazil**	7	17	30.0	EBX Group
Stefan Persson **Sweden**	8	31	26.0	H&M
Li Ka shing **Hong Kong,** **Canada**	9	15	25.5	Cheung Kong Holdings
Karl Albrecht **Germany**	10	8	25.4	Aldi

Top ten 2013

Name	This Year Rank	Over All Rank	Wealth USD Bil'	Source(S) Of Wealth
Carlos Slim Mexico	1	3	73.0	Telmex, América Móvil, Grupo Carso
Bill Gates United States	2	1	67.0	Microsoft
Amancio Ortega Spain	3	5	57.0	Inditex Group
Warren Buffett United States	4	2	53.5	Berkshire Hathaway
Larry Ellison United States	5	4	43.0	Oracle Corporation
Charles Koch United States	6	21	34.0	Koch Industries
David Koch United States	7	22	34.0	Koch Industries
Li Ka shing Hong Kong, Canada	8	15	31.0	Cheung Kong Holdings
Liliane Bettencourt & family France	9	29	30.0	L'Oréal
Bernard Arnault France	10	7	29.0	LVMH Moët Hennessy • Louis Vuitton

Top ten 2014

Name	This Year Rank	Over All Rank	Wealth USD Bil'	Source(S) Of Wealth
Bill Gates	1	1	76.0	Microsoft
Carlos Slim Mexico	2	3	72.0	Telmex, América Móvil, Grupo Carso
Amancio Ortega Spain	3	5	64.0	Inditex Group
Warren Buffett United States	4	2	58.2	Berkshire Hathaway
Larry Ellison United States	5	4	48.0	Oracle Corporation
Charles Koch United States	6	21	40.0	Koch Industries
David Koch United States	7	22	40.0	Koch Industries
Sheldon Adelson United States	8	23	38.0	Las Vegas Sands
Christy Walton & family United States	9	24	36.7	Wal-Mart
Jim Walton United States	10	14	34.7	Wal-Mart

About The Author

S. A. Nantembelele holds a Bachelor of Commerce in accounting (B.com – Accounting) from University of Dar Es Salaam. Having successful in small businesses he has built a strong base knowledge of business and interpreneurship.

S. A. Nantembelele has written several dozen of articles about business, interpreneurship and motivation. He has also written few self publishing books in last year.

S. A Nantembelele has one lovery and caring beautful wife and no children to date.

www.ingramcontent.com/pod-product-compliance
Lightning Source LLC
Chambersburg PA
CBHW070817180526
45168CB00002B/644